Raising Families

Envisioning the Church to Empower its Neighbourhood

Raising Families

Envisioning the Church to Empower its Neighbourhood

By Alan Cutting

Copyright

Scriptures taken from the Holy Bible, NEW INTERNATIONAL VERSION® Anglicised, NIV® Copyright © 1979, 1984, 2011 by Biblica, Inc.® Used by permission. All rights reserved worldwide.

Scriptures taken from the NEW AMERICAN STANDARD BIBLE (R), Copyright (C) 1960, 1962, 1963, 1968, 1971, 1972, 1973, 1975, 1977, 1995 by The Lockman Foundation. Used by permission.

Scripture taken from THE MESSAGE: THE BIBLE IN CONTEMPORARY ENGLISH, copyright©1993, 1994, 1995, 1996, 2000, 2001, 2002. Used by permission of NavPress Publishing Group.

Contents

Acknowledgements

As a young pastor and member of a church planting team based in the UK, I soon learned the folly of considering church to be merely a matter of what happened in a church meeting and in a church building. As our churches gained a greater understanding and confidence as to *why* God had placed us in the locations in which we served, we found ourselves being more and more involved with the everyday lives of our neighbourhoods.

This was the vision and approach that I took into my international work with *Raising Families*. But in working out these values and priorities in the incredibly diverse cultural contexts of so many marginalised communities around the world, I needed a lot of help. Many went before me, others travelled with me, and still more will follow, all bringing their enriching wisdom and perspectives.

Many colleagues and friends - Nic Balbutski, Simon Barrington, Chris and Jodi Blackham, Rev Malcom Duncan, Tim Holmes, Rev Francis Karemera, Deborah Randall, Archbishop Onesphore Rwaje, Rev Wandy Shongwe, Mellbin Simangolwa and Irina Trofimova among them - have invested enormous amounts of prayer, passion, wisdom, resource, strategy and intelligence into the development of the *Raising Families* programme. Some planted. Some watered. But God gave the growth.

I have learned a lot from each and every one of them, and I am very grateful for their guidance, correction, support and encouragement over the past few years.

"I always pray with joy because of your partnership in the gospel from the first day until now, being confident of this, that he who began a good work in you will carry it on to completion until the day of Christ Jesus." Philippians 1:4.

I am also very grateful to Samaritan's Purse UK for its patient and generous investment into the *Raising Families* programme, and to my diligent editors and proof readers, Kathy Morrison and Charles Claydon.

Introduction

During my decade and a half with Samaritan's Purse, firstly as an employee and now as a consultant, it has been my great privilege and joy to work alongside thousands of local churches around the world. A few are big, urban and influential, but the vast majority are tiny, situated way off the beaten track, and forgotten. But whether they are located in Africa, Eastern Europe or in Central or South East Asia, I have discovered that many of them have some great things in common. They want to engage meaningfully with their society, unite across confessions, lead many people to Christ, and see holistic transformation in the lives of the poorest and most marginalised families in their communities.

Since 2012 I have managed a programme called *Raising Families*. It is what is often called a 'Church and Community Mobilisation' (CCM) programme, and it does exactly that. It mobilises churches and communities. It is a great example of a church-based programme that is committed both to social action *and* to seeing dozens of people coming to Christ every week. Not one or the other, but both.

In managing the *Raising Families* programme, I have been able to work alongside several thousand churches around the world, envisioning, encouraging and mobilising them to make a genuinely transforming impact upon their neighbourhoods. Whilst having a global model, *Raising Families* (or *RaFa*, as it is affectionately known, at least in English speaking countries) is tailored to be appropriate to each diverse social, economic and regulatory culture and context. Pastors have been envisioned, and churches have been mobilised. The programme has functioned very successfully through experienced partners in Central Asia and in Africa since 2006.

The model that underpins the programme has always been designed to be self-sustaining and, to this day, even years after the formal training in some locations was completed, hundreds of churches remain committed to this holistic, faith-filled vision of integral mission. Also, as I write, other mission agencies and NGOs are looking to adopt the model, and develop it in other countries around the world.

Since the programme scaled up in 2012, *Raising Families* has actively served 3,002 local churches from many denominations, strengthening those churches in the *proclamation* and the *demonstration* of the gospel of Jesus Christ. Denominations and churches that had previously competed with one another have learned how to work together in harmony for the sake of the Kingdom of God. And those 3,002 churches have each been tasked with supporting and mentoring twenty of the most vulnerable families in their neighbourhood, over a period of three years.

In earlier years, I had the great privilege of planting and pastoring some extraordinarily dynamic churches in the UK, and have since served churches and communities in many dozens of countries around the world.[1] However, for me to manage the *Raising Families* programme has been the most fulfilling, significant and effective role that I have had in almost fifty years of Christian service.

The studies in this book are an attempt to outline some of the core values and practices that have underpinned the *Raising Families* programme. Each chapter typically includes an introductory section, a biblical rationale, the *Raising Families* context, and some quotes and testimonies from *RaFa* practitioners. Finally, they offer some questions suitable for individual contemplation or for small group discussion.

The book is written with a UK Christian readership in mind, and it is anticipated that through these studies, UK church leaders and activists who have an interest in exploring some of the lessons being learned by churches in other parts of the world will be stimulated in their own determination to engage in new, meaningful and Christ-like ways with their own UK communities.

---

[1] You can read my life story and travels in my book *Cutting Across the Borders* ISBN 978-1-7200-2050-9

With some good preparation done by group leaders, and as long as each chapter is read by group members before the group meets, the twelve chapters of this book quite naturally create a three month curriculum for small groups that meet weekly. Alternatively, each chapter can be used individually and without reference to the others.

And should you and your church wish to explore and contextualise these values and practices further, I am available for the leading or facilitating of events such as a church weekend or a training series. Contact me through my website, CuttingAcross.com.

Glossary

BBI   Bridge Builders International

CAG   Church Action Group

CCMP   Church and Community Mobilisation Process

CIA   Central Intelligence Agency

CIDOS   Change, Impact, Design, Organisation and Sustainability

CIP   Continuous Improvement Process

DRC   Democratic Republic of Congo

EU   European Union

HRA   Human Rights Awareness

IDP   Internally Displaced Persons

LQAS   Lot Quality Assurance Sampling

LRA   Lord's Resistance Army

M&E   Monitoring and Evaluation

NGO   Non-Governmental Organisation

OVC   Orphans and Vulnerable Children

RaFa   Raising Families

RWF   Rwandan Francs

S&L   Savings and Loans

SDGs   Sustainable Development Goals

TB   Tuberculosis

UN   United Nations

Study One

Community Engagement

The role of the church in the community

Jesus Moved Into Our Neighbourhood

"Oh Mum, do I *have* to go to church this morning?"

"Yes son, you must!"

"But Mum. It's so *boring!*"

"Son, you *must* go, and that's an end to it."

"But *why* Mum?"

"Because you're 43 and you are the pastor."

So goes the old joke.

So maybe I'm not the only one who has become restless with the endless habit of 'going to church'. Since coming to Christ as a child, personally, genuinely, wonderfully, miraculously, I guess I've made my way to church on a Sunday fifty times a year, or five hundred times a decade. With other similar meetings probably doubling or even trebling that number, I guess you could call me a regular church goer!

Going to church. I need it, I believe in it, and I genuinely value it. But it can often still make me feel quite frustrated and uninspired. Actually, what I need, believe in and genuinely value is not *going* to church, but *belonging* to a local church, and all that this entails. It's about meaningful discipleship and about collective worship. It's about covenant community and, most definitely, it's about effective and outward-looking mission. So if 'church' is merely perceived to be an outdated barn of a building, or even a diary of endless meetings held *in* an outdated barn of a building, something tells me we are being seriously short changed. The scripture does *not* say, 'Jesus came that we might have meetings, and might have them more abundantly'. We need an outlet!

We've all heard why the Dead Sea is called the Dead Sea. Apparently it's because no water flows out of it. It just slops around gathering salt. Pillars of the stuff; almost ten times the amount of salt as is in the ocean. It is so salty that plants and animals struggle to survive around it. And, without seeking to get *too* gloomy with the analogy, it is the lowest place on earth. I really don't fancy being a member of the Dead Sea Christian Fellowship.

This is not the picture John painted for us when he said, *"The Word became flesh and blood, and moved into the neighbourhood"* (John 1:14 The Message). Here we have an engaged, relevant, connected, vibrant environment, with Christ at the centre and mission to its community at its heart. This is the church that I want to be a part of.

Jesus explained to His disciples that it wasn't just Him that had moved into the neighbourhood, but that they (and we) were also to be salt and light in the public arena (Matthew 5:13-16). Then, before He returned to His Father, the resurrected Jesus told His disciples that as the Father had sent Him, i.e. into the community, even so He sent them (John 20:21).

Dreams, Doors and Disappointments

The bible speaks of the whole of creation waiting with eager longing for the revealing of the sons of God (Romans 8:19).

One hot night in May 2011 I slept in a rural hotel not far from Stakhanov in the Luhansk Oblast of Eastern Ukraine. The hotel, which actually had no name, was merely the top floor of a struggling five-storey medical centre. The trees surrounding the building were so tall and so close that there was still no view as such from the curtain-less fifth floor windows. With its simple rooms, rough furnishings and creaking bathroom, it cost about £8 to stay for one night.

I had spent much of the previous day with Sergey, a very interesting local pastor. He had vision and apprehension in equal measure. He dynamically explained to me that there were the same number of evangelicals in Ukraine as there were people living with HIV and AIDS, and so in theory the Church should be able to care for each and every one of them. Indeed, 30% of the membership of his own church had been addicts. But he was also frustrated. "The world wants the church to help, but it doesn't want to listen. The church wants the world to listen, but it doesn't want to help", he said.

Now I'm not given to regular visions, but I recall very clearly the dream that God gave me that night. In my dream, I was back at the very church building I'd visited the previous day. It looked quite similar to the little tin hut mission buildings you can occasionally still see in rural areas of the UK, with its green painted corrugated iron walls and a door clinically placed under the apex of the front gable end. Gathered outside, clustered along the path to the entrance, were various members of the local community. People of all ages; some, families, some elderly, some children. There was a palpable atmosphere of anticipation as they crowded expectantly around the front door. They were chattering vibrantly with one another, expressing excitement that at last something exceptional was about to happen in their community. The sons of God were about to be revealed. The Christians were about to emerge from the building, and bring Good News to the community. 'Our prisoners will be released.

Our sick will be healed. Our relationships will be restored. Our problems will be over!'

But as time went by, no-one emerged from the little tin building. The sound of muffled voices, and occasionally singing, could be heard inside, but the door remained firmly shut. Gradually the conversations of those waiting outside began to fade, and then dwindled altogether. Shoulders dropped. One by one, and with great disappointment, people turned and walked away, until there was no-one waiting outside.

That was it. Despite the warm, summer, early morning sun that was streaming, albeit dappled into my room through those tall trees, I woke with a terrible heaviness; a real sense of sadness. Was that real? No, it was a dream. But what was God saying to me through this dream? Was this really a criticism of this particular church which had kindly hosted my visit just the day before, or of its Pastor Sergey, with his genuine and compassionate heart for its neighbourhood? I really don't think so. I could only conclude that the dream was just a sad symbol of what is actually happening with thousands of churches around the world.

It has always intrigued me to see how different church confessions demonstrate their values, priorities and beliefs by the architecture and furniture of their buildings. The positioning of the cross, the height of the pulpit, the screens that link (or disconnect) the priesthood and the laity, the centrality of the communion table, the comfort levels of the seating, the size of the PA system. They all say a lot. Early that morning I concluded that for me the most important piece of church architecture is the front door, and maybe Psalm 87:2 ("The Lord loves the gates of Zion") suggests that I'm in good company. And I determined again to encourage the church to become community- rather than buildings-based.

The whole of creation waits with eager longing for the revealing of the sons of God. Or, as the Phillips version of the bible translates Romans 8:19, "The whole creation is on tiptoe to see the wonderful sight of the sons of God coming into their own." Let's not disappoint them anymore.

The Raising Families Context

Raising Families encourages the local church to spill out from the safe shell of its buildings and the quotidian of its meetings, and to embrace a new and outward paradigm. It urges the 'Community of the Redeemed' to find new and effective ways of engaging with its neighbourhood, so that the world may see that Jesus is the Son of God who is alive and who loves them, and so that along with the wider community *all* can prosper.

"Seek the peace and prosperity of the city to which I have carried you... Pray to the Lord for it, because if it prospers, you too will prosper." Jeremiah 29:7 NIV

Through an envisioning process, the churches we work with discover how to become more integrated with their society, meeting with local authorities and other agencies, and learning how to present themselves as a genuine, intelligent and practical resource for the service of the community at large. Church Action Groups are formed that, in cooperation and collaboration with other local authorities, commit to working with twenty of the most vulnerable families in their neighbourhood over a three year period.

"I used to have a vision for a bigger church. Now I have a vision for a better community." *Pastor in Kyrgyzstan, after being envisioned with the Raising Families approach.*

Raising Families churches constantly testify as to how their relationships with their neighbours have been practically, radically and positively transformed. They also tell of how their confidence levels have rapidly increased through gaining an understanding of how their community works, through undertaking simple needs- and asset- assessments, and through learning skills that the community needs, whether that means learning how to prune the fruit trees for a better yield, how to work creatively with children with disabilities, or how to advocate for and access better health care.

On the basis of monitoring and evaluation already conducted on all six of the programmes completed in Africa and Central Asia since 2015, and due 100% to the blessing and favour of God, we can gratefully report that we have partnered with 3,002 churches and 59,681 families. Each of these families has seen significant, practical, quantifiable improvements to their life; sickness averted, children in school, crops in the field and food on the table. And what is more, a total of 14,705 people have reportedly come through repentance and faith into a living relationship with God through Jesus Christ.

And long after the formal *Raising Families* three year programme ends in a particular location, these Christ- and community-focussed churches continue to engage with their neighbours, working with still more vulnerable families, and envisioning and equipping churches of different confessions and in neighbouring villages on how to turn themselves 'inside out' for the sake of the gospel.[2]

The Community Engagement Spectrum Exercise

We use the following exercise (or similar alternatives) in the *Raising Families* envisioning process, to enable church leaders and activists to see some of the different styles of churches that exist around us today. You are welcome to use it or adapt it for your own purposes, i.e. at a training day or church weekend. It really needs 20-30 people to make it work well.

Purpose of the exercise

Through light-hearted sketches, the leader facilitates learning from the group itself, enabling them to act out and articulate for themselves some of the typical approaches to mission and

---

[2] For example, the CIDOS post-CCMP review conducted by Bridge Builders International in Swaziland (September 2016) reported that "a minimum of eighteen months after all external trainings and mentoring have ended, 95% of the churches continue to function as holistic developers of the most vulnerable families in their communities. The majority of these report that they are 'thriving', maintaining a 'clearly recognisable model' to the one they first learned through *Raising Families*, that the work has been 'transformational' for the participating families, and that it has 'greatly influenced the vision, values and priorities of their church'. What is more, 69% of these groups has birthed at least one more group in their locality."

community-engagement they might have encountered in different types of churches. As an outcome, the leader facilitates the group in encouraging a shift across the spectrum towards the fifth group, which is the *Raising Families* or 'development' approach.

Activity

Divide into five groups of 5-6 people each, giving them 15 minutes to prepare a five-minute light-hearted sketch which typify and illustrate one of the five following approaches to local church (each group prepares a sketch of a different approach): 'Inward', 'Word-only', 'Attractional', 'Aid' and 'Development', based on the paragraphs below. Ensure that one or two people with development experience are placed in the 'development' group, as this one will be the most challenging group to model. Careful and sensitive placing of those participants who are not so familiar with church will realistically and inclusively enable them to act out the roles of 'newcomers'.

When the sketches have been played out in front of the whole group, ask each group how they approached the exercise and what they learned from it. Ask those watching the sketches what they noticed and what they felt about what they'd seen. Whilst being faithful to the purpose of the session, the facilitator should be careful to find some positive things to say about each of the five approaches (e.g. they could be described as 'the Prayers', 'the Preachers', 'the Welcomers', 'the Activists' and 'the Enablers').

Group 1: The 'Set Apart' (Praying) Approach

The church that sees itself as set apart and holy, and which locks itself away in its buildings, and makes no (or only occasional and fearful) connections with the outside world. Think about the language it uses, its strengths and weaknesses, what its values are, what it prays for, how it interacts with the world (when it occasionally has to), and how it interacts with other Christians (if it ever has to).

Group 2: The 'Word-Only' (Preaching) Approach

The church that wants to see more people saved, but that sees its mandate as only verbal; to preach, rather than to be involved in any actions of kindness or good work. Think about the words it uses, the positive and negative impact of the way it communicates with outsiders, how outsiders would react to this words-only approach, and how the church would respond when faced with extreme poverty, or the urgent need to engage in social action.

Group 3: The 'Attractional' (Welcoming) Approach

The church that wants to be welcoming to others, but only functions or operates within its own buildings and meetings, therefore only has a vision for welcoming outsiders into their own environment. Think about how different its world would seem to a newcomer, what they would be expected to understand and the behaviours they would have to fit into should they attend their meetings, and what sort of welcome they would receive. Maybe not everyone inside would be welcoming, and maybe not everyone outside would be welcome.

Group 4: The 'Aid' (Activist) Approach

The church that sees its mandate as reaching out to the whole person; body, soul and spirit, and is ready to speak and act in the community as well as from their church buildings, but limits its social action to programmes that *give things away* and *does things for people*, rather than developing people into maturity and self-sustainability. Think positively about some of the things it could provide and do, but also think about the limitations of an aid approach. Think also about how beneficiaries would feel in the long term about purely being the recipients of hand-outs, and think about some of the attitudes that can develop and problems that can occur when people in the neighbourhood become dependent on the church's activities and provisions.

Group 5: The 'Development' (Enabling) Approach

The church that, like the one above, sees its mandate as reaching out with an integral mission to the whole person; body, soul and spirit, and is ready to act within the community as well as from their church buildings base, but which also has a real understanding of the need to empower and develop people – offering a hand-up rather than a hand-out. Think positively about how it leads people to Christ, how it disciples, empowers and develops people and communities, how it uses its resources, what challenges it faces, what it says no to (i.e. what it *won't* do), how and at what levels it engages with its society (e.g. who it partners with), and how it determines root problems and solutions.

Testimonies from Raising Families Practitioners

Shining in the Community

"*Raising Families* is the programme of the church that helps us shine in the community. The believer has been transformed, and now fulfils his mandate in his environment. We are family-focussed because this is a fundamental building block of our society. To do this we have to deal with several issues, e.g. housing, relationships, work ethics etc. This way we preach the gospel and let our light shine around the community, so they see God and come to Him." *Church Action Group member, Rwanda.*

Becoming Practical about the Gospel

"Our church now not only offers worship services. *Raising Families* has taught us to become very practical. We have a savings group which consists of 20 people, some from the church and some from the community, but all of whom contribute 200 RWF (17p) per week. We decided to save until December and then shared out the proceeds but, to make the savings grow, we all invested into beans. These will sell for a much better price in September. So we aim to have enough money by next December for each person in the savings group to buy a goat. We've just started allowing people to borrow from the savings, making it a savings and loans group. We charge 5% interest on the loans, and not one person has so far failed to replay."

"We meet every Monday. First we all dig the garden of our host for the week, then we collect our savings together, then we share the Word of God and pray for each other. If people cannot afford to save 200 RWF then they put in 50 or 100, and they will receive a proportional amount back in December. But the interest will be shared evenly to all savers. Our next step is to ensure that everyone in the savings group manages to purchase health insurance (*the fundamental requirement for accessing health care in Rwanda*). But, however practical it is, *Raising Families* has actually helped bring much spiritual growth to our church. Husbands firstly watched whilst their wives got involved, then they liked what they saw and asked to join in. In this way husbands have come to church, and then go on to have their marriages blessed and formalised." *Church Action Group leader, Rwanda.*

Beautiful Hope

Pastor Samson's community was a very difficult place to live. There was a heavy sense of pain there. HIV was rampant and was rapidly taking lives. This was the way of life for this community. Residents started to become accustomed to the trauma and suffering that was so obvious, so pressing. "The consequence of this rampant HIV is that many of the adults have died, leaving orphaned children behind. We have approximately 892 orphans here. Every single weekend we had at least 6 to 7 funerals for parents being buried. Our community burial ground is completely full." Some of the older children around 18 years old had to lead their homes without any other adult present at all. Malnourishment and disease among the children was a huge problem.

When the *Raising Families* programme began in the community, Samaritan's Purse worked with Pastor Samson and his church, inspiring them through scriptural and practical teaching to reach out to their community to meet their needs. "We were able to fully understand the depth of the real problems in our community. We discovered that we were able to do something about it. We were taught how to identify the most vulnerable in our community and how to address them and engage the church."

Pastor Samson knew that the children were the ones most affected and that the church together could help them. "We started talking to three other churches in our community. Together we decided that we wanted to adopt a group of 54 children. Our plan was to take the most vulnerable and put them into families and allocate dedicated, trained caregivers to every group of 7 children." The churches used the knowledge they gained from *Raising Families* training to grow maize, beans and sweet potato. They built up sustainable resources through small livelihoods to purchase food, cooking pots and utensils for the children. "We have been able to keep all these children healthy and strong. Malnutrition has been eradicated completely from our community. We no longer have hungry children and disease has reduced drastically. People are talking with hope again!" The *Raising Families* scheme has been nicknamed 'Thembelilhe' by the community, which means 'Beautiful Hope'.

"He will wipe away every tear from their eyes. There will be no more death, or mourning or crying or pain, for the old order of things has passed away," (Revelation 21:4). *Local church pastor, Swaziland.*

Questions for Group Discussion

- Why do you think God has chosen to plant a church in our particular neighbourhood?
- What words do you think describe the way our church is perceived in its neighbourhood?
    - By our immediate neighbours
    - By the poorest in our community
    - By other community-based agencies
    - By local authorities
- How do you know this? What makes you answer in this way? Have you asked them?
- In what ways could our church move more naturally into its neighbourhood?
- If our church was to engage more practically in the community, what do you anticipate the *spiritual* impact would be?
- Share some key scriptures that convince you of
    - God's heart for the poor
    - The role of the church in the community
- How well do our church members understand the way our community hangs together?
- Who are our community's key stakeholders and influencers, and how can we as a church engage with them better?

- Which other locally-based social agencies, churches and community initiatives have skills that we could learn from and with whom we could find either partnership or cooperation, to the benefit of the poorest in our community?

- What are our community's main needs, and what are its main assets?

- What ideas and initiatives for transformation can our church offer its neighbourhood?

- What proportion of our church members are genuinely ready to express their love for Jesus by both proclaiming *and* demonstrating His love in their neighbourhoods?

- What can be done to turn passive church-goers into activists?

- How can we make use of our church buildings, vehicles etc to turn them into effective resources for the whole community and not just for the church members?

- Does our church have a small group structure (home groups etc) and if so, what is its community-based mandate? In what ways could these groups learn together how to give their lives away to their neighbourhoods?

Study Two

Integral Mission

Presenting the whole gospel of Jesus

Proclamation and Demonstration

"Preach the gospel at all times. If necessary, use words." This saying, or others very similar to it, have become very popular to quote in the last couple of decades. It is usually accredited to St Francis of Assisi, the founder of the Franciscan Order. But one thing always puzzled me about this quote. If he said it approximately eight hundred years ago (he died in 1226), and I've been listening to sermons for over fifty years, why had I never heard it until about twenty or so years ago? Could it be more to do with the spirit of our age than it has to do with the quote itself?

In fact, it is very doubtful that St Francis did ever say this. Glenn T Stanton, who researches these things, suggests the closest he came to uttering these words was in his Rule of 1221, Chapter XII, when he emphasises *how* the Franciscans should practice their preaching. "No brother should preach contrary to the form and regulations of the holy Church nor unless he has been permitted by his minister ... All the Friars ... should preach by their deeds."[3]

And according to Mark Galli of *Christianity Today*, Francis actually used a *lot* of words to proclaim the gospel. He preached in the Assisi church of Saint George, and later in the cathedral of Saint Rufinus. He often preached on Sundays, spending Saturday evenings devoted to prayer and meditation, reflecting on what he would say to the people the next day. When he travelled, he could be found "sometimes preaching in up to five villages a day, often outdoors. In the country, Francis often spoke from a bale of straw or a granary doorway. In town, he would climb on a box or up steps in a public building. He preached to . . . any who gathered to hear the strange but fiery little preacher from Assisi. He was sometimes so animated and passionate in his delivery that his feet moved as if he were dancing."

So what do I mean by 'the spirit of our age'? Well, I fear that since the turn of the 21st century a pendulum has swung, and an imbalance has taken place. So keen are we to be authentic in our *demonstration* of the gospel, that we have lost the art and the determination to *proclaim* the gospel. I see this in the life of everyday Christian believers, and even in the rationale of some local churches. And it is also evident in the practices of some of our valued partner mission and NGO agencies in the world of

---

[3] https://www.thegospelcoalition.org/article/factchecker-misquoting-francis-of-assisi

'Church and Community Mobilisation', even though they talk a lot about having an 'integral mission' approach (i.e. the gospel impacting every area of our lives). Excellent as their programmes are, and learn from them as I sincerely do, I am sometimes left surprised and disappointed by the way many of them hold back when it comes to the need to equip the church for the *proclamation* of the gospel within their programmes.

I sense that for a couple of decades the church has (very necessarily) had to think long and hard about ensuring that its actions are compatible with the gospel it proclaims. In this respect, we can learn a lot from the nineteenth century Evangelicals, who pioneered much of the social action that was implemented towards the abolition of slavery, and for the improvement of health and educational, prison reform and vulnerable children's welfare. And, albeit in more *subtle* and often *local* ways, we can clearly see that the Church is also influencing *today's* society with a wave of practical, compassionate Christian initiatives that have very positively impacted communities around the world. Food banks, debt counselling and support groups for the elderly are typical programmes of many local churches. David Cameron's domestic policy of 'Big Society' (2010-13) leant very heavily on the good will of local churches to do things in their communities that he knew no politicians could have hoped to achieve.

However, whilst we have made great progress in *demonstrating* our gospel, the same probably cannot be said for *proclaiming* it. I beg you, please prove me wrong, but right now I don't honestly think it is within the expectation, or maybe even the capability, of most church-goers to confidently lead someone to Christ. Pause for a second and take that in, for it is a shocking confession.

It seems to me that the parts of our society that currently speak the loudest, e.g. through the media and popular culture, have totally abandoned God and are deeply, cynically secular. I collected several topical examples specifically for this chapter, but then I thought, "Why give them even *more* airtime?"

However, my point is this. As a result of this secularism we have become reticent to *talk* about sin and its consequences, and to *proclaim* the good news of salvation in Jesus Christ, for fear of being perceived as exclusive, bigoted or something-phobic. We have become unwilling to rock the boat of political correctness and social acceptability, instead leaving the proclamation of the gospel to a few brave experts who we call evangelists. This has meant that many of our neighbours, work colleagues and relatives – *most* of whom actually in their heart of hearts have very little sympathy with what the media tells us is now normal and to be celebrated - have been denied the opportunity to discover Jesus for themselves.

It is one thing for us to *live* in a way that helps people *observe* the impact of the gospel, and even to be impressed, but it's another thing to *speak* in a way that helps people *respond* to Jesus personally and actually walks that journey with them from darkness into light, today. Your *actions* set it all up wonderfully, but your *words* rarely bang it home. We need both the deeds and the words. As Paul said, *"How then will they call on the one they have not believed in? And how can they believe in the one of whom they have not heard? And how can they hear without someone preaching to them?"* (Romans 10:14).

"The essential key to move us beyond the polarisation between *evangelism* and *social action* is love. Love compels me to respond to another human being in need. I have no hidden agenda to use the response as bait to evangelise, nor do I respond to simply manifest the Kingdom. I respond because I *love*. Similarly, I share the Good News of Jesus and call people to follow Him because I love them and know that life in Christ *is* life. Wanting the very best for each person made in the image of God means ensuring they have the opportunity to know Christ." *Sheryl Haw, International Director, Micah Global*

I suggest that this is the time to be amazingly, publicly *proud* once more of Jesus and His gospel, to talk *confidently* of the love, power, grace and mercy of Jesus, as well as of the *'offensiveness'* of the cross, and to hone our skills at verbally engaging with those around us and, with compassion and with clarity, bringing them to the point of decision, for the sake of the gospel.

The Biblical Rationale

OK, 'Integral mission' is not directly a biblical phrase. But there again, neither are 'evangelism', 'missional communities', 'home groups' and 'revival', and we've used all of them often enough. Integral mission, or holistic mission, is a term coined in Spanish as *misión integral* in the 1970s by members of the evangelical group Latin American Theological Fellowship (or FTL, its Spanish acronym) to describe an understanding of Christian mission which embraces both evangelism and social responsibility. The International Congress on World Evangelization in Lausanne in 1974, and The Micah Network coalition in September 2001 have done a lot to establish both an understanding of the concept and an awareness of its implications.

The Micah Declaration on Integral Mission states, "Integral mission or holistic transformation is the proclamation and demonstration of the gospel. It is not simply that evangelism and social involvement are to be done alongside each other. Rather, in integral mission our proclamation has social consequences as we call people to love and repentance in all areas of life. And our social involvement has evangelistic consequences as we bear witness to the transforming grace of Jesus Christ."

The mission of Jesus and the early church was truly integral. One Sabbath day, as was His custom, Jesus went to the synagogue in Nazareth, where He had been brought up. He stood up and, quoting from Isaiah 61, He said, *"The Spirit of the Lord is on me, because he has anointed me to proclaim good news to the poor. He has sent me to proclaim freedom for the prisoners and recovery of sight for the blind, to set the oppressed free, to proclaim the year of the Lord's favour."*[4] Then He rolled up the scroll, gave it back to the attendant and sat down, ready to teach. The wide eyes of everyone in the synagogue were fastened on Him, and a shiver of anticipation and expectation went down their spines as He looked up and told them, *"Today, this scripture is fulfilled in your hearing"* (Luke 4:16-21). In other slightly amplified words, Jesus was simply saying, "My Father and I are interested in *everything*; every aspect of your lives, be it your salvation, your health, your education, your livelihood, your home, your protection, your hobbies. There is no *person* that we do not love and want the very best for, be it the poor, the prisoner, the blind or the oppressed. And what's more, we are interested in every

---

[4] Note that in this brief and very practical discourse, Jesus still used the word 'proclaim' three times.

aspect of your *society*, be it its justice, its politics, its social structures, its arts, its culture, its economy."

But it is not merely the comfortable companionship of *proclamation* and *demonstration* (word and deed) that we are considering here. It is the *whole of life* that needs this practical and spiritual integration. Our *gospel* can only become integral if our own *lives* are integral. We know from Romans 8:28 that *"in all things God works for the good of those who love him, who have been called according to his purpose."* Not just in spiritual things (whatever they are!), but in *all* things.

We know that through Jesus *all things* were made (John 1:3), that the Father placed *all things* under His control (John 13:3), and that *all things* were committed to Him by the Father (Luke 10:22). Jesus also talked about the restoration or the renewal of *all things* (Matt 17:11, 19:28). We read in Ephesians that He fills *everything* in *every way* (Ephesians 1:23), and that one day *all things* will be united in Him (Ephesians 1:10). Throughout the epistles we read this same expression. It is rewarding to do a simple New Testament bible study based on the expression 'all things', whilst focussing on the fact that God and His Kingdom wants to, and needs to, and *does* (whether we want it to or not) impact every area of our lives. This is *wonderful* news for those who have laid their whole lives down before Jesus. But it's rather scary news for those who quietly determine to hold parts of their life back in the darkness. All things!

Micah 6:8 summarises integral mission wonderfully, giving us three key words which outline what the Lord requires of us, not just personally, but also in our relationships, and in our role within society. All in one scripture! *"With what shall I come before the Lord and bow down before the exalted God? Shall I come before him with burned offerings, with calves a year old? Will the Lord be pleased with thousands of rams, with ten thousand rivers of oil? Shall I offer my firstborn for my transgression, the fruit of my body for the sin of my soul? He has shown all you people what is good. And what does the Lord require of you? To act justly (do justice), and to love mercy (kindness), and to walk humbly with your God."*

Between the ages of 25-40, as a pastor, husband and father, I heard God speak to me - regularly, specifically and clearly - about major issues in my life. God specifically told me

- To commit to taking my family to Australia for a month when I had less than £11 in the bank
- Which house to move into
- In which town to plant a church
- Even the church building He wanted us to buy

In each case, I saw God's prophetic word confirmed miraculously and without manipulation.

Then this 'hot line to heaven' just stopped. Had something gone badly wrong? A good friend and wise mentor told me not to worry. "When you were a child," he said, "you had to be told exactly what to do. Now you are growing up. You need to understand God's heart, His values, His purposes, His priorities, and make more decisions on the basis of these."

I see this maturing process happening for Micah as he worshipped the Lord. "How can I please you Lord? I love you so much I could give you burned offerings (like Moses did). I could lavish gifts upon you (like David did). I love you so much, I could even sacrifice my most precious inheritance (my firstborn, just like Abraham did). My loveliest, my most, my influence, my closest! All for you! You are worth it. I so want to be right with you and close to you. Is this what you want me to do?"

But then he thinks again. He thinks again of what he has learned about God; His heart, His values, His nature, His purposes, and His priorities. And then, knocking his fist against his head in confession of his own slowness to learn, he speaks once more, this time to himself:

"He has shown you, O man, what is good. And what does the Lord require of you but to do justice (act justly), to love mercy (kindness, or loyalty), and to walk humbly with your God."

This is the commission of the church, and of every believer. It is an invitation to please God (by doing what is "required" of us) through

- An *action.* To *do* justice: in the way we engage with society

- An *attitude*. To *love* mercy: in the way we treat one another
- A *journey*. To *walk* humbly: in the way we relate to Him

Leadership theorist and academic John Adair hints towards a similar integral triangle in his Action Centred Leadership tool, where he refers to the need to balance "the task, the team, and the individual".

Healthy churches need to contend with these three aspects of our life in Christ and try to hold them in healthy balance. Each church has its strengths, emphasis, focus, and each has its weaknesses and blind spots, but here is a diet for a healthy and integrated church - the 'Community of the Redeemed'.

1 Do justice - the public task of the church in society

This is the *action*. Justice means 'social righteousness'; the church being involved in, integrated with, loving its community - being salt (flavouring and preserving what is good), and light (shining in the darkness, so that people may see their good actions and glorify the Father in heaven).

However, in our engagement with society, individually, and as churches, we can very easily fall into one of two errors. Either we become disengaged or we become conformed.

When we become disengaged, we are neither *in* the world nor *of* it. We become so separate from the culture that we embrace the language and lifestyle of a ghetto, or enclave (developing an inward-looking, defensive, siege mentality) and do not engage comfortably with those around us. Rather than the hospital, the school and the army that it's meant to be, church for us eventually becomes merely a club.

When we become conformed, we are both *in* the world *and* of it. We are so determined to engage with society that we become conformed to its values, and become indistinguishable from the people we are trying to reach. We become so absorbed by the culture that we become identified by it, and lose our distinctiveness and prophetic edge. Rather than the worship, discipleship and mentoring environment that it's meant to be, church for us eventually becomes an irrelevance.

Doing justice is the public task of the church in society, and enables us to stay relevant, appropriate, purposeful, compassionate and prophetic.

2 Love kindness - the spirit of the church in its relationships

This is the *attitude* - of kindness, or mercy, or loyalty. These are such simple, almost twee expressions, and yet so profound.

"Comfort, comfort my people, says your God. Speak kindly *to Jerusalem. Call out to her that her warfare has ended, her iniquity has been removed, and she has received from the Lord's hand double for all her sins."* Isaiah 40:1-2.

"Don't think lightly of the riches of his kindness and forbearance and patience. It was the kindness of God that led us to repentance." Romans 2:4.

Raising Families encourages churches to work diligently at being kind to one another. Church can so easily be reduced to a series of meetings. Long meetings and abundant meetings! Loving kindness rescues the church from becoming a thin diet of meetings, and turns it into a warm family and an effective team.

Some bible versions use the words 'kindness' and 'mercy' interchangeably. If *grace* is God abundantly giving us what we *don't* deserve (i.e. His love), *mercy* is God withholding from us what we *do* deserve (i.e. His judgement). The church is to show the same mercy in its relationships.

3 Walk humbly - the journey each believer undertakes with the Father

This is the *journey*. It is our determination not to abandon our 'L' plates, and to remain hungry to learn. The journey is a walk of continual brokenness, of letting God strip away the arrogance of our hearts.

Walking humbly with God, personally, will save us from becoming a "horizontal" or merely a "social" community, and will welcome the presence of God into everything we are, and everything we do.

Jeremiah 9:23-24 (NIV) states something very similar. *"'Let not the wise boast of their wisdom or the strong boast of their strength or the rich boast of their riches, but let those who boast boast about this: that they understand and know me, that I am the Lord, who exercises* kindness, justice *and* righteousness *on earth, for in these I delight,' declares the Lord."* Humility (boasting in the right things), kindness (or mercy) and justice (or righteousness).

And this journey of intimacy through humility, this attitude of relationship and this action of justice is a theme that can be seen again at the end of Isaiah 19 ("The oracle concerning Egypt"). In an interesting parallel to the Micah scripture, Isaiah talks of a highway from Egypt to Assyria, and prophesies that *"In that day Israel will be the third party with Egypt and Assyria, a blessing in the midst of the earth, whom the LORD of hosts has blessed, saying, "Blessed is Egypt My people, and Assyria the work of My hands, and Israel My inheritance.""* Isaiah 19:24-25 (NASB). What the Lord requires of each of us (as in Micah) is the same as He has provided for the nations. Egypt is My people (relationship), Assyria is the work of My hands (action), and Israel is My inheritance (humble worship, intimate belonging), says the Lord.

And a final word from Micah Network. "If we ignore the world we betray the word of God, which sends us out to serve the world. If we ignore the word of God we have nothing to bring to the world. Justice and justification by faith, worship and political action, the spiritual and the material, personal change and structural change belong together. As in the life of Jesus, being, doing and saying are at the heart of our integral task."[5]

The Raising Families Context

In my time with Samaritan's Purse, I have loved to work alongside local churches around the world that want to engage meaningfully with their society, and see holistic transformation in the lives of the poorest and most marginalised families in their communities.

Raising Families does exactly that. It has functioned successfully through experienced partners in Central Asia and in Africa since 2006, strengthening churches from many denominations in the proclamation and demonstration of the gospel of Jesus Christ. Whilst having a global model, *Raising Families* is tailored to be appropriate to each social, economic and regulatory culture and context.

Raising Families churches can clearly evidence measurable, practical transformation in neighbouring families' health, education, livelihoods, shelter and protection, as they seek to address the felt needs of their communities....

---

[5] http://www.micahnetwork.org/integral-mission

- Physically (or practically, i.e. addressing issues of health and livelihoods)
- Spiritually (helping hundreds of people come into a personal relationship with God through Jesus Christ)
- Emotionally (helping people come to a place of peace with their own identity and personality)
- Socially (helping people find peace in their meaningful relationships)
- Societally (helping people access a place of justice and respect in the broader community)

The rationale of this programme is based on a belief that as the main agent of the Kingdom of God on earth, the local church has been appointed by God to fulfil a compassionate, Christ-centred mission to its community and neighbourhood. In order to equip the church for this task, *Raising Families* offers a simple, practical framework of envisioning, encouragement, training, mentoring and support. Through this process we have seen many churches fulfilling The Great Commission (Matthew 28:19-20). However, not only do they make many disciples, but they also demonstrate the whole gospel that Jesus proclaimed in the synagogue in Nazareth (Luke 4:18-19), i.e. the lifting of people from poverty, be it spiritually, physically (i.e. in terms of health and livelihoods), emotionally, relationally (or socially) and societally.

Raising Families moves churches along the following practical continua:

- From being buildings-based to *community*-based
- From releasing individual activists to equipping *teams* of activists
- Turning 'dreams' into *plans*, and 'visions' into *strategies*
- From being aid- or charity-focused into becoming *development* or *discipleship* focused
- From a programmatic (or project) approach to a *relational* approach
- From thinking dualistically (in parallel) into thinking *holistically* (proclamation and demonstration)

So how does it work? Samaritan's Purse would seek and fund national partners. These are Christians of proven leadership capacity in the church and community, women and men who have a clear vision for the values and practices of the *Raising Families* programme. These national partners provide envisioning and training to local church leaders, who then decide whether or not they wish to pursue this approach. Those who do will select active members from their church who form a Church Action Group (CAG). These CAGs firstly assess both the needs and the assets of their community, and then commit to working with a minimum of twenty of their most vulnerable neighbouring families, supporting and facilitating their development in terms of health, education, livelihoods, shelter and protection. In some countries we have worked with as few as 20 churches at a time. In others we work with over 700 churches. Consequently, over the last six years, 59,681 families had directly benefitted from this programme. Sometimes broader, more general community activities and interventions such as environmental clean ups, providing access to markets, schools and health services, improving water supplies etc become significant by-products of this process. But at its core, *Raising Families* is about each church supporting and empowering twenty of the most vulnerable families in their locality to see significant, practical, quantifiable improvements to their lives: sickness averted, children in school, crops in the field and food on the table.

The national partners always function under a registered agency such as an NGO or a National Denomination, through which we can ensure good governance and accountability. The programme is underpinned in each country by an agreed logical framework, and monitored and accounted for monthly by means of activity tracking, and with quarterly financial returns and six-monthly benchmarking and results monitoring.

The intelligent commitment of lead bishops and pastors within the participating denominations, and the provision of excellent facilitators have proved to be key components for the success of the programme. Delivering excellent value for money, *Raising Families* works so well because it is a prayer- and bible-based programme, locally owned and implemented by the church and its neighbours, and relies not on external hand-outs, but on resources already available in the community.

Testimonies from Raising Families Practitioners

Many pastors tell us that *Raising Families* has had a big impact on the thinking and values of their church, and has been a means of growth in terms of their numbers, their reputation, their influence, their unity and their connectedness with their society.

Here are some quotes from church leaders and activists who now think differently about the gospel:

"We used to think narrowly about being Christians – just spirituality – but now we also train on such things as 'society in God's eyes', 'having a holistic approach', and we deliver practical sessions about problem analysis, team building, project development, advocacy and leadership. Last night we invited someone in to teach us on nutrition." *A pastor in Central Asia.*

"Thank you for all the trainings you have given us. I used to think God was only spiritual but now I see a whole gospel. We provide advocacy for children's education and their fathers' employment. We have seen 32 new believers because of our work in the last two years. In the previous two years, 15-20 came to Christ. So by doing things differently, and by serving the community, we have seen almost twice as many people saved." *A pastor in Central Asia.*

"Our Action Group started work about twelve months ago, with monthly trainings and food distributions. The team has been motivated to serve poor people and share the gospel with them. Previously they said they saw no results from merely preaching the gospel, and people just got scared when they tried, but now they report that they are more effective and more compassionate." *A pastor in Central Asia.*

"This is a totally new way of presenting the gospel! God gives us big joy, because it's better to give than to receive. We had heard that scripture so often, but now we really feel the joy!" *A pastor in Central Asia.*

"I was once invited to a conference in Manila where they talked about the interaction of words and deeds in the gospel, and the need to combine them practically. I was fascinated, but I struggled to fully understand it, so I read books, studied at university, and when doing my masters at Edinburgh University in 1990, my thesis was on 'How to integrate words and deeds – the cohesion of evangelism and social action'. And then to Kigali in 2011, and helping us to make sense of this within the whole of the Anglican Church, came the Samaritan's Purse *Raising Families* programme, although I prefer to call it a process rather than programme, as this will go on long after Samaritan's Purse has left." *The former Archbishop of L'Eglise Anglicane au Rwanda.*

"This programme is amazing! We are really excited to be in a *Raising Families* relationship with The Anglican Church. This is the meaning of the Cross – bringing us together across denominations. We are deeply committed to the ministry and philosophy of integral mission; word and deed together. We have tussled with this question; "How can the church be the centre not just of spiritual development but also of social and community development?" And so we love this programme. Do you know what I like about it most? It makes things possible. It brings hope." *The former Executive Secretary of the Association of Baptist Churches of Rwanda.*

"We've done evangelism and done it quite well, but we've not been great on discipleship. Now we see the close interaction between discipleship and development, and this has helped us remarkably. It's another aspect of revival – the community sitting up and taking note. Our churches used to expect us pastors to do everything for them, whereas now the main reason they visit the pastor is to tell him what they themselves are doing." *Senior pastor in the Anglican Church of Rwanda.*

"We understand that our cell groups, committees, or action groups - you call them missional communities - are the foundational building block of the local church. It's them that practically expresses the life of Christ within us, be it helping people back to God, repairing their houses, supporting savings and loans groups etc. We are learning not to be anxious about anything, but in every situation, by prayer and petition, with thanksgiving, to present our requests to God." *Archdeacon in the Anglican Church of Rwanda.*

"Since the training on integral mission we've seen a lot of transformation. People are discovering their gifts and using them. Many who deserted the church are returning due to these activities. Due to the work of this group we have seen more baptisms and confirmations." *A pastor in Swaziland.*

Questions for Group Discussion

- Which scriptures would you use to describe the holistic nature of Jesus' mission?
- How integral (or holistic) is the ministry of our church?
- In what ways do we serve our community physically, spiritually, emotionally, socially, societally?
- Which other churches in our neighbourhood could we partner with in this integral mission?
- What would have to change (in terms of our priorities, our attitudes and our lifestyle) for us to commit to working with twenty of the most vulnerable families in our neighbourhood to see holistic transformation over the next three years?
- Paul said that he saw his task in Christ as *"leading the Gentiles to obey God by what I have* said *and* done, by the

power *of signs and wonders, through the power of the Spirit of God."* (Romans 15:18-19 NIV). Again, in 1 Thessalonians 1:5 (NIV), he said, *"our gospel came to you not simply with* words *but also with* power, *with the Holy Spirit and with deep conviction. You know how we* lived *among you for your sake."* This study has focussed on *proclamation* (our words) and *demonstration* (our deeds), but isn't there something still missing? Shall we call it *manifestation* (God's power)? Could it be that we have been trying to ride a tricycle on only two wheels?

- Discuss together this all-important third aspect of integral mission that Paul speaks of in these verses, and finish by praying together that our words, our lives *and* the power of God might be more evident in our own lives, and in the life of our church, and in the lives of the churches linked to *Raising Families* around the world.

Study Three

Unity with a Purpose

When churches and believers work together

Let There Be Love

On my travels around the world, I am often asked to comment on the state of the Church in the UK. Now in truth, my awareness of the state of the Church in the UK is extremely limited, and I don't seek to set myself up as its spokesman. But one of the replies I offer to this question, albeit merely a generalism, goes something like this.

"Well, comparably speaking, the Church in the UK isn't huge in numbers, but some good things are happening within it. For example, a generation or two ago believers and local churches were much more entrenched in their own denominations, their own dogma, and their own ways of doing things. It was unusual for believers to meet or work together across their confessional lines. However, these days, most regular believers are not nearly so conscious of their differences, or protective of their own denominations, but are happy to meet together, pray together and work together for the sake of Jesus."

Of course, I do see this healthy and united outlook in many other countries as well, but sadly this cannot be said for every part of the world. Many of the churches of Eastern Europe and Central Asia suffered greatly during the Soviet era and, as a survival strategy, many tended to implode into their shells. This led to many small churches embracing a siege mentality, and to occupying the next seventy years of their time with quite private meetings in their homes and chapels. To their great credit, many survived, although when in 1990 glasnost (openness) and perestroika (restructuring) became the buzz words, a large number of the brave survivors of the protestant church culturally looked and sounded like they had emerged from a previous century. But with the enemy at the door, without an outlet, and with minimal checks, balances and wisdom from the wider Christian church, their isolated world had got smaller and smaller. What do you do for seven decades of seclusion, other than to go over and over the nuances of fine doctrine and Christian practice, justifying them through more and more obscure interpretations of scripture, until you believe that only you and your congregation have the truth, and all others are to be mistrusted or refuted? All these years later, a number of these local churches are still not only terrified of being tainted by 'the world', but are also very cautious in their approach towards other believers, and quick to find fault both in the values of others, and in the way they do things. Attempts to unite churches (for which nothing major really need divide them) still require enormous patience, and are often met with mistrust and division based on the tiniest and sometimes most bizarre of issues.

I hardly dare tell you this shocking story, but it's true. It was in Tiraspol, Prednistrovye (Eastern Moldova) where a young pastor told me of his attempts to encourage other pastors in the city to pray together. One older pastor whom he visited responded extremely cautiously and, in an attempt to see whether or not his soul would be compromised by praying with his guest, asked the younger man what is probably the most bizarre (and creepiest) question I've ever heard. "Before I decide whether or not we should pray together, I need to ask you in what position you sleep with your wife".

I also have a very similar story to tell you but, thankfully, one which has a much more positive ending. It is the story of a young couple who, immediately after marrying, were sent by their big church in a Central Asian capital city into a small town many miles away. There they were commissioned to plant a church. The novice twenty year old pastor decided to visit the three other pastors in the town to ask if they could all pray together. "No, of course not," came the hostile reply. "We'll pray *for* you, that you will see the error of your ways, but we'll not pray *with* you."

Disappointed but undeterred, the young couple set about serving God and their community, and God blessed them in wonderful ways. Fourteen years later they were asked by *Raising Families* to head up the work in their region, and then in their country. The couple, by now in their mid-thirties, invited these same pastors to an 'envisioning' meeting, where they outlined the vision and purpose of the *Raising Families* programme, and its potential impact on the community they were all a part of.

Despite it being a relatively small town with very few believers, this was the first time any of them had ever been in one room together. Before the meeting they sat silently, pretending to read their bibles or to scribble meaningless notes on a pad, whilst waiting for the formalities to begin. The start of the meeting was tense, and eye contact was non-existent. But God did something wonderful in that one simple meeting, and by the time it ended they had prayed together, each pastor had exchanged their cell phone numbers with the others, and they had committed to a brave and extensive ministry to the many homeless people in their town!

That was eight years ago, and these pastors remain firm friends. They share meals together, borrow each other's cars, speak in each other's churches, and have even taken all their young sons together on a couple of 'dad and lad' 700km road and fishing trips to the neighbouring country. For the ministry to which they committed on Day One, each pastor uses their specific gifts and resources so that together they provide one cohesive service to the homeless, one of the most challenging groups of people in their neighbourhood. Many men and some women have been saved, delivered, rehabilitated from alcohol and drug abuse, clothed, housed, employed, and are now living in their right minds.

This is not only unity. It is unity with a purpose.

Task and relationship must grow together. They are like a boot on each foot. Too many steps with one without the other one keeping up will result in the splits, and we've had far too many of them in the Church! Churches can possibly undertake a week long mission (task) together without too much angst, as long as they can then scurry back into their comfort zones when it finishes! However, attempting a long term or continuous task without relationship is ultimately doomed to failure. But equally, relationship without a task will also eventually implode into a mushy clique of frustration, or worse. The words 'devil', 'work' and 'idle hands' rush rather hastily to mind.

Together with the churches I planted years ago, I used to really enjoy this song:

Let there be love shared among us,
Let there be love in our eyes,
May now Your love sweep this nation,
Cause us O Lord to arise.

Give us a fresh understanding

Of brotherly love that is real.

Let there be love shared among us,

Let there be love.[6]

We bravely looked into each other's eyes as we sang it together. But ultimately, what do you *do* with all this loving feeling? How can our love for one another glorify Jesus? Unless it is tangibly demonstrated somehow, through lives laid down for Him, for each other and for our communities, all we'll end up doing is giving each other tear-filled hugs and sickly grins.

The Biblical Rationale

"How good and pleasant it is when God's people live together in unity!" wrote King David in Psalm 133:1 NIV.

David knew all about unity, expressed through covenant friendship. His relationship with Jonathan is a great example of such relationships, where two parties commit to one another (1 Samuel 18:1-4) and, in essence, say, "If you are ever in need, never forget that I have laid down all other options but to respond to you in activity of compassion" (1 Samuel 20:4).

And David also knew how to knock up an army out of *"all those who were in distress or in debt or discontented"* (1 Samuel 22:2

---

[6] Dave Bilbrough © 1979 Thankyou Music

NIV). He *"shepherded them with integrity of heart; with skilful hands he led them"* (Psalm 78:72 NIV). As their commander, David had a strong and united bond with those who became his army's chief men. They really were amazing chaps. One killed eight hundred of their enemies in one encounter, and another three hundred. Another stood his ground and struck down the Philistines until his hand froze to his sword. And still another one went down into a pit on a snowy day and killed a lion! These lads definitely showed potential!

But one night during harvest time David and his men were resting in the cave of Adullam. The cave was separated from Bethlehem by the opposing Philistine army, but David, longing for water, said in the hearing of his thirty chief warriors but to no-one in particular, *"Oh, that someone would get me a drink of water from the well near the gate of Bethlehem!"* (2 Samuel 23:15 NIV). It was just like that craving for Marmite that most people have encountered one week into their first short-term mission trip to darkest somewhere-or-other!

Twenty seven of the chief men chuckled at the irony and impossibility of it, and agreed how wonderful it would be to taste that sweet water from home. However, unnoticed, and with a nod and a wink, the remaining three men quietly slipped out of the cave, quickly devising a plan as they went. They crept down into the Valley of Rephaim, broke right through the line of dozing Philistines, drew some water from the well near the gate of

Bethlehem and, being careful not to spill their precious cargo, broke back through the Philistine lines again, up through the valley, back into the cave, and presented David with their random act of kindness!

The final irony was that David wouldn't drink it, but instead poured it out as a love offering to the Lord. *"Far be it from me, Lord, to do this!"* he cried. *"Is it not the blood of men who went at the risk of their lives?"* (2 Samuel 23:17 NIV). David had thirty 'chief' men (Heb. *rosh*, meaning *heads*, or *leaders*), but he only had three who were called 'mighty' (Heb. *gibbor*, meaning *great, strong, champions*). A chief man will do what is commanded of him. He will lead well and be bold in battle. He will even kill lions in pits on snowy days. But mighty men are even harder to come by. They will love, they will initiate, and they will be ready to lay down their lives for the sake of another. The difference between chief men and mighty men is a glass of water. Their unity has purpose.

And so into the New Testament. The most precious, extensive and profound prayers of Jesus are recorded in John 17. What an amazing privilege it is for us to be given this insight into the relationship Jesus has with his Father! This 'High Priestly Prayer' outlines their relationship and the glory they share. Although it is a glimpse into the perfect and eternal harmony of heaven, much of their prayer is actually for the world or, more accurately, for those whom the Father rescued from the world and gave to Jesus (v6-8). That's us – the Church! Jesus prayed for our protection, our joy, and our sanctification (v 9-19). And specifically, beautifully, incredibly, He asked His Father *"that all of them may be one, just as you are in me and I am in you. I have given them the glory that you gave me, that they may be one as we are one – I in them and you in me – so that they may be brought to complete unity"* (John 17:21-23 NIV).

I've been at pains in this chapter to stress that our unity is for a purpose. So here comes the purpose in John 17: *"....that they may be perfected in unity, so that the world may know that you sent me, and loved them, even as you have loved me"* (John 17:23 NIV). Far be it from me to claim a complete understanding of what Jesus was praying here, but I sense a link here between the perfection of unity and the world coming to know the love of God. *"That the world may know..."* This is the purpose and the reason for our unity. Jesus prayed that we might have unity, with a purpose.

"...make my joy complete by being like-minded, having the same love, being one in spirit and of one mind." Paul, in Philippians 2:2 NIV

Paul tells us that Christ Himself is our peace, and that it is He who has made us one and has destroyed the *"dividing wall of hostility"* (Ephesians 2:14 NIV). He goes on to urge the church of Ephesus to *"preserve the unity of the Spirit"* (Ephesians 4:3 NASB) and instructs their leaders to *"equip his people for works of service, so that the body of Christ may be built up, until we all reach unity in the faith"* (Ephesians 4:12-13 NIV). Note the order here. Unity of Spirit. Works of service. Unity of faith. We may not all agree with the nuance of every doctrine and practice of the church down the road, and they may not agree with all of ours, but in the meantime we are all required to maintain the unity of the Spirit *and* fulfil the works of service together until (or before) we all reach the unity of faith.

Finally, we see the link once more between unity and purpose in Paul's writing to the church in Corinth:

"Therefore, if anyone is in Christ, the new creation has come: the old has gone, the new is here! All this is from God, who reconciled us to himself through Christ and gave us the ministry of reconciliation: that God was reconciling the world to himself in Christ, not counting people's sins against them. And he has committed to us the message of reconciliation. We are therefore Christ's ambassadors, as though God were making his appeal through us" (2 Corinthians 5:17-20 NIV).

Christ has reconciled us, and given us the message, or ministry, of reconciliation. Now that we have been reconciled, we have become reconcilers. We are gatherers, not dividers. We bring peace, not turmoil. We are ambassadors, not aggressors. We are reconcilers, not alienators. And if I am in covenant with God, and you are in covenant with God, then like it or not, my friend, we are in covenant with one another.

The Raising Families Context

Undertaking social action together enables churches to build trust together. We have found that churches that don't have great historic trust in one another can still come together, not on the basis of theological debate but on the common needs of their community. As they work together they build trust, relationship and love for one another and find that their doctrinal differences take on a different and less polarised place in their priorities. Social action helps normalise inter-church relations. Their hard work puts a lot of things in perspective.

Every Saturday during the Soviet era, public workers were forced to 'volunteer' their time to undertake public duties such as cleaning the streets, repairing public amenities or disposing of the rubbish. This 'compulsory volunteerism' would take place on a Saturday and was called '*subbotnik*'. It will not come as too much of a surprise, therefore, that the concept of 'volunteerism' still creates a sour taste in the mouths of many. However, after the first *Raising Families* programme was rolled out to the churches in a big town in Central Asia (churches that live under the constant albeit random threat of violence and persecution), they heard about the value of attempting a 'seed project', this being a simple manageable task that they could do in the community, which would help them gain confidence and raise their profile in the public arena.

As one group of eight churches they nervously sought and were given low-level permission to do a *'subbotnik'* style clean-up of the city's tired and scruffy central park, which overlooked the local authority offices. When the City Mayor happened to look out of his window one Saturday morning, he saw about sixty men, women and children hard at work, sharing tools, laughing, singing, and doing a great job. The park hadn't looked so good in years. Going out to investigate, and looking authoritative, he went up to the nearest of the workers.

"Who are you?" he asked.

"We're the church" came the slightly nervous reply.

"Which church?" he asked.

"Just the church."

The mayor probed further. "Doesn't it have a name?"

Hesitantly the willing worker shrugged his shoulders. "It's just the church" he said, "The church in our town."

"Well who's in charge?" asked the Mayor.

Nervously the group facilitator stepped forward, not sure what her punishment was going to be. But to her relief and joy the Mayor started clapping his hands and with a big smile said, "I have never seen such a hard working team. What's your secret? You all look like you *want* to be here! Bring three of your poorest team members to my office on Monday morning, and I will give them all employment!"

Three paid jobs from one morning's work! And from the encouragement of that experience of working together, once a month on a Sunday morning for the last eight years, those eight churches in that city have abandoned their own congregational plans and come together to worship God. Their Action Group has birthed several others and, years after the formal end of the *Raising Families* programme, continues to serve compassionately and harmoniously throughout their city.

Raising Families crosses confessional borders in almost all our countries of operation. Only in Rwanda did we originally have a programme which was managed entirely through one denomination. This is the Anglican Church, which has successfully completed two three-year programme cycles. Anecdotally we had heard of many of their Church Action Groups birthing other groups in neighbouring villages, and virtually always these seemed to be working with other confessions. And so when we planned a third programme, which started in 2016, His Grace the Archbishop worked hard to ensure that the Anglican Church formally partnered with the Baptist Association and the Presbyterian Church, and provided their experienced facilitators to become mentors to those of the other denominations, each of which is now working well with one hundred of their local churches. Their united efforts have been recognised as a wonderful contribution to the post-genocide rebuilding of this beautiful 'Land of a Thousand Hills'.

Testimonies from Raising Families Practitioners

"We are really excited to be in relationship with The Anglican Church in this Samaritan's Purse-funded programme. This is the meaning of the Cross – bringing us together across denominations. When our Anglican brothers came with this offer we thought, "This is amazing!" Firstly we looked for good leaders – this is the key – people who are passionate for the work and have good leadership skills. From those we selected, one is a pastor with finance and divinity degrees, and the other is a youth pastor. Secondly we looked for our church networks and communities which had the right circumstances, and came up with one in the east and one in the west. The churches in these regions are strong and growing." *Executive Secretary of the Association of Baptist Churches of Rwanda.*

"We have appointed two coordinators, one in Zinga and the other in Gitamara. The Anglican and Presbyterian Churches are really sisters. It is great news that we are working together." *Vice-President of Eglise Presbyterienne au Rwanda.*

"Our local authorities used to think churches were always fighting against each other for the sake of more members. Now they encourage people to go to church because of their service in the community." *A pastor in Swaziland.*

Questions for Group Discussion

- Think of conversations you have had with Christians of a different theological persuasion to your own, and discuss the atmosphere of those meetings. Were they polite; warm; natural?
- If so, what made them so? If not, could they have been? What attitudes, assumptions and expectations could have made them more comfortable?
- Think of times when your church has partnered with others for the sake of outreach events, missions or community service, and discuss how successful these initiatives were.
- Did all parties feel it was a fulfilling experience? Why (or why not)?

- Would you do it again, and if so, would you do the same things and in the same way?
- What happened to the inter-church relationship after the events or the programme ended?
- What stops churches in your area from copying those churches in Central Asia which abandon their own meetings once a month and meet as the city's one church for worship, teaching and fellowship?
- If they did, what would be the advantages, and what could be built?
- What could the challenges be, and what would it take to overcome them?
- Why do you think that most interdenominational initiatives that do happen come under a separate charity or church-neutral identity? Is this necessary and is it helpful? Does that let the church get away with not having to bother about working out its unity with others?
- What are the 'absolutes' that would cause you to refuse to partner with another church?
- If you felt you couldn't quite 'partner' with another group (either another church or another agency in the community), what words would you use to describe other levels of credible and positive relationship (e.g. collaboration, agreement, cooperation, communication)? What would each of these examples mean in practice?

Study Four

The Aid and Development Spectrum

The appropriate use of both

Two Ends of the Same Stick

One of my previous line managers was vastly experienced in community development in rural Africa. I often recall him, albeit very graciously, lamenting the sad outcome of a UK church initiative which was to send a couple of containers of second hand clothes to the village he had lived and worked in. "I'm sure it wasn't their *intention* to put two local tailors out of work. They just didn't think."

Aid is instant. It is usually visual. It tangibly meets today's need and, let's be honest, it often makes the donor feel quite good about themselves. Job done. Sorted. I've done my bit. But as the root cause has not been addressed, tomorrow the need will be staring us in the face once more.

So what happens when I give aid repeatedly, to the same beneficiaries? What happens to the work ethic of those who receive it? What happens to their dignity, their self-esteem?

How can the recipient of my aid develop their own skills and talents, when I've done things *to* them and *for* them rather than *with* them? And what happens when my funds run out, or I get bored and move on to whatever has now captured my attention?

Robert Lupton, in his hard hitting book *Toxic Charity* (2012), offers his readers what he calls an 'Oath for Compassionate Service', which commits to the following six attitudes.

1. I will never do for others what they have (or could have) the capacity to do for themselves.
2. I will limit one-way giving to emergency situations.
3. I will seek ways to empower through employment, lending, and investing, using grants sparingly to reinforce achievements.
4. I will put the interests of the poor above my own (or organisation's) self-interest, even when it means setting aside my own agenda.
5. I will listen closely to those I seek to help, especially to what is not being said – unspoken feelings may contain essential clues to effective service.
6. Above all, to the best of my ability, I will do no harm.

In qualifying the second of these oaths he uses a great quote:

- Give once and you elicit appreciation.
- Give twice and you create anticipation.
- Give three times and you create expectation.

- Give four times and it becomes entitlement.
- Give five times and you establish dependency.[7]

Aid and development can at first glance appear to be very similar, whereas in fact they face in entirely opposite directions. If you like, they are two ends of the same stick. One gives and the other equips. One offers a hand out and the other offers a hand up. One masks the problem and the other solves it. One holds onto the power and the other gives it away. One creates dependency and the other establishes sustainability. The orphanage is (hopefully) better than the street, but fostering and training biological families on parenting skills and relationships is a whole lot better still. The food bank protects from hunger today, but equipping people to generate their own crops and income is much more likely to solve the problem of food insecurity. Distributing clothes will keep people warm *this* winter, but savings and loan groups will help clothe them in the long term.

It is rather a sweeping statement, but in general terms I would suggest that the church thinks 'aid' 80% of the time and 'development' maybe 20%, whereas I believe it would do a lot better to completely reverse that statistic. Yes of course, let's give 'aid' when it is essential for the immediate maintenance of life and protection (say 20% of the time), and let's give it with an

---

[7] Toxic Charity: How Churches and Charities Hurt Those They Help, And How to Reverse It by Robert Lupton ISBN 9780062076205

overwhelmingly generous heart. But equally, let's offer 'development' wherever there is the opportunity to equip, mentor, develop and maximise people's capacity to become responsible, functioning, capable members of society (say 80% of the time). This will be more complex, more costly in time, and require us to learn new skills and embrace new and much deeper relationships. Crucially, it will also require us to lay down the hidden reins of power and control, which are so dreadfully imbalanced in the donor's favour when it comes to the distribution of aid. With aid we can remain relatively detached, getting away with talking quite clinically about having 'beneficiaries', 'recipients', or 'service users'. With development the relationships are more balanced, more complex, and more integrated. We have 'colleagues', 'partners', even 'friends'. Paul actually went a whole step further, by saying, *"Even if you had ten thousand guardians in Christ, you do not have many fathers, for in Christ Jesus I became your* father *through the gospel"* (1 Corinthians 4:15).

You might have noticed in the previous paragraph that I didn't use the expression 'maximise people's *independence'*. That's because I believe Western society has elevated the concept of independence well beyond that which is God's plan, consequently damaging the interconnectedness of community, and fostering individualism and harsh rights-based relationships. Our obsession with making independence our goal has isolated many people on lonely and fragmented islands. By all means let's help people move from dependence, but *through* independence and on into the wholeness of interdependence, where we all responsibly use our talents, gifts and resources for the benefit of one another in a harmonious society.

It is not only the mentor or discipler or 'developer' who has to commit to the complexities and challenges of change. It is also the one being mentored who, depending on their circumstances, will quite possibly have to lay down attitudes of laziness, blame and irresponsibility.

I was a pastor and church planter for more than twenty years during the final quarter of the twentieth century, but at an early age I had determined not to fit into the mould of what it appeared to me that some Christians thought a pastor should be, i.e. he who was employed to maintain their equilibrium. When something bad happened, the pastor was expected to pray or guide the flock back to how things were before. She or he was merely there just to keep things ticking over and keep people out of trouble, comforting them when things went wrong. But the concept of a pastor being there to mentor, equip, grow, build or change anything was a little too radical for some people. I doubt very much I would have stuck with it if I was forced to adhere to a mandate of merely maintaining the status quo.

God's intention is not only that we are cared for and protected in the vulnerability of our present state (which He does anyway and with such mercy), but also that we become mature, attaining to the whole measure of the fullness of Christ.

The Biblical Rationale

The bible speaks repeatedly of the importance of giving to the poor.

Moses commanded Israel to store tithes, *"so that the Levites … the foreigners, the fatherless and the widows who live in your towns may come and eat and be satisfied, and so that the Lord your God may bless you in all the work of your hands"* (Deuteronomy 14:28-29 NIV).

Isaiah prophetically declared that the fast the Lord had chosen was to *"share your food with the hungry and to provide the poor wanderer with shelter – when you see the naked, to clothe them, and not to turn away from your own flesh and blood"* (Isaiah 58:7 NIV).

James (1:27 NIV) tells us that one of the marks of the *"religion that God our Father accepts as pure and faultless is … to look after orphans and widows in their distress."*

Jesus went a very challenging stage further, using our preparedness to give aid (or not) as an illustration of what will separate people when He comes in glory. *"Then the King will say to those on his right, "Come, you who are blessed by my Father; take your inheritance, the kingdom prepared for you since the creation of the world. For I was hungry and you gave me something to eat, I was thirsty and you gave me something to drink, I was a stranger and you invited me in, I needed clothes and you clothed me, I was ill and you looked after me, I was in prison and you came to visit me. Truly I tell you, whatever you did for one of the least of these brothers and sisters of mine, you did for me"* (Matthew 25:34-40 NIV).

We could label these acts of mercy as 'hand-outs', but this sounds unnecessarily patronising to me. Or 'relief', which possibly sounds a bit clinical. For the purposes of this study, let's call them 'aid'.

"The righteous have freely scattered their gifts to the poor, their righteousness endures for ever; their horn will be lifted high in honour" (Psalm 112:9 NIV). Aid offered with a pure heart is precious and is beautiful. It expects nothing in return. It helps keep people alive. It is a kiss from Jesus - the day it rained in colour in Greytown. It reflects the *mercy* and the *kindness* of God. And it is not only for those in real need in the *church*, but equally for those in real need in the community.

What is not so often recognised is that the bible also speaks of an appropriate time for enabling 'development'. We should think of this in the same way as we think of discipleship: the developing of people. Whereas discipleship could be considered to be a service

79

towards those who already belong to Christ, development is the service of the church to *all* of mankind, and particularly for those in our societies who are vulnerable. In the same way as justice is sometimes referred to as 'social righteousness', development could also be called 'social discipleship'. It is the equipping of interconnected people and communities to stand on their own feet, and to become architects of their own destiny.

In fact, I would be bold enough to suggest that this development/discipleship approach is the framework in which the *whole* of scripture is set; the mechanism by which the goal of all history will be accomplished, and the reason why God has placed your church in its community. I find the book of Ephesians particularly helpful. *"In all wisdom and insight he made known to us the mystery of his will, according to his kind intention which he purposed in him with a view to an administration suitable to the fullness of the times, that is, the summing up of all things in Christ, things in the heavens and things upon the earth"* (Ephesians 1:8b-10 NASB). Paul then reminds us (Ephesians 2:10 NIV) that *"we are God's workmanship, created in Christ Jesus to do good works, which God prepared in advance for us to do."* And he teaches in Ephesians 4:11-13 NIV, *"Christ himself gave the apostles, the prophets, the evangelists, the pastors and teachers, to equip his people for works of service, so that the body of Christ may be built up until we all reach unity in the faith and in the knowledge of the Son of God and become mature, attaining to the whole measure of the fulness of Christ"*. Here we have God's ultimate purpose (the summing up of all things in Christ), who we are in Him (God's workmanship), what we're here to do (good works), and how we should go about doing it (equipping his people for works of service).

The parable of the bags of gold (or the parable of the talents) has the same intrinsic principles of growth, maturity and discipleship as Paul outlines in Ephesians, only not exclusively in the church, but also in the community. Through trust, respect, faith and a good work ethic, two of the servants featured in this story made use of the resources their master had given them, whereas the third did nothing with them, other than bury them in the ground. When the master returned, he praised the two for generating more resources, and rebuked the third for his laziness (Matthew 25:14-30).

Why do you think that Jesus, who knew all things, is recorded in the four gospels as asking an amazing 173 questions? Who touched me? Who do *you* say that I am? Do you *want* to get well? Do you *love* me? Jesus didn't just give answers but also asked questions in order to mature the thinking and practice of those around Him (Matthew 20:21, 32, Luke 18:35-43, John 5:5-9). He didn't always provide for people Himself, but sometimes asked others to provide (Luke 9:12-13). And He concerned Himself with the whole state of those He met (Matthew 11:4-5, Luke 4:16-21), not purely their 'spiritual' state. Moreover, this wasn't a mentoring method addressed exclusively to His disciples; it was His approach to everyone He encountered.

The early church was well used to giving aid in emergency situations. Cornelius (Acts 10:4) and the Macedonian Church (2 Corinthians 8:2) were praised, and the Churches of Antioch (Acts 11:27-30) and Corinth (2 Corinthians 8:7) were urged on in these matters. But one can quite easily sense hints of the tensions that had already been caused when aid had been given too liberally or inappropriately. In the giving of aid, the early church leaders faced challenging issues relating to fairness, expectation and selection. It wasn't long before the Hellenistic Jews complained against the Hebraic Jews because their widows were being overlooked in the daily distribution of food (Acts 6:1). In 1 Timothy 5 Paul outlines which widows should receive support and why. He urged Timothy to ensure that proper recognition was given to those widows who were *really* in need (3, 16). If a widow had children or grandchildren (4), or was not over sixty (9, 11), then Paul was much tougher, even warning younger widows against idleness (13) and talking nonsense (13). Again in Titus 3:14, Paul's instruction to the church was to provide for *"urgent needs"*, i.e. not just randomly for 'needs'.

The Raising Families Context

Raising Families churches work very hard at caring for the vulnerable poor in their neighbourhoods, particularly with the frail-elderly and the disabled. They can regularly be found building simple homes for them, tending to their land and providing food, clothing and day services. But this is only a part of their work in the community. The main work is to walk with vulnerable families and households through and *out* of their poverty, imparting knowledge and skills to enable these families to be the designers of their own lives.

Development techniques are used wherever possible. The vulnerable families we work with are encouraged to embrace a glass half full 'asset based' approach. In other words, they are taught to focus on what they *have* got, not upon what they *haven't* got. They are encouraged to work together to maximise the resources of their village, be it land, or time, or knowledge and skills, and maybe even access to influential people. Income generating initiatives and savings and loans schemes are introduced as early as possible in the process.

Even where a little aid is given, it is always given with the determined mindset of when and how can this be turned round into development. If our actions lead us nearer to dependency, then we are moving in the wrong direction. Consequently (and our donors often ask us about this) the funds we raise for *Raising Families* go almost exclusively into supporting the facilitators and trainers and mentors, not into buying 'chickens and goats', or clothes or food, to distribute to the poor. And no longer do we send short-term teams of British people to put a roof on a building or paint a wall, as though the local work-force was incapable of such actions. Those who do visit go to encourage and learn from our brothers and sisters.

Hand-outs given by *Raising Families* churches to vulnerable families in the community are not entirely unknown, but they are rare. They are more likely to be given

- when relationships (and therefore trust) are first being built
- as random acts of kindness
- when the need is so urgent and critical as to be a matter of life or death
- where people will never realistically be able to improve their own state, due to them (e.g.) living with serious mental ill health or a learning disability, or being frail elderly etc (*"the poor you will always have with you"* (Matthew 26:11 NIV)); or
- when the church has simply yet to fully grasp the difference between aid and development.

Particularly in regions where there has been a significant NGO presence and the injection of much aid, breaking the dependency culture is an even bigger challenge, and often in such places the envisioning stages of our training takes longer. Our facilitators regularly have to battle against the dubious practices of certain NGOs such as the giving of 'sitting allowances', i.e. cash paid to local people to attend their trainings. As a consequence, I quite often receive stories of pastors and churches who come to participate in the *RaFa* training with an expectation of a hand-out so firmly lodged in their mind that they drop away in disillusionment when they realise no such hand-out is forthcoming. Others 'get it' but only after some struggles.

Testimonies from Raising Families Practitioners

We don't want their handouts any more

Thusi Malinga from Mbelekweni in Swaziland tells of the battles his own communities had with this aid verses development tension:

"For many years our community had a lot of very poor people, and we always expected NGOs and the government to come and solve our problems. We had committees for receiving donations and committees that applied for donations. We had committees that "set-up" people to be eligible for grants and food support. The community had become an NGO community because almost everyone benefited from what we thought was our resourceful wisdom."

"As a result the community members no longer farmed their land as much, and people were getting bored and troublesome. Selfish petty materialism was the order of the day. We had many quarrels around who got what and what went to whom. Even our chief and his cronies were involved and his homestead had been used for hoarding bags of grain and food handouts from the UN and other major international organisations. Our young people had also joined in and many claimed to be orphaned, yet they had guardians that took reasonable care of them in extended families. We had lost our moral fibre and God's name was being mentioned less and less. Our young girls were becoming pregnant as they got a benefit if they proved that they had no child support. People deliberately allowed things to fall apart so that they would qualify for and receive relief aid. A lot of this aid was being sold cheap to neighbouring communities for hard cash."

"Some of us knew that our community was in deep trouble, but we just could not give-up the endless stream of handouts that we received almost monthly. In December 2014 we received about 100 tons of soya mince product from an American donor. Every household got more than its reasonable share. This soya ended up being fed to the chickens as chicken feed. We just did not realise that what we perceived as wealth and good fortune was actually the worst form of poverty. Things had become desperate and chaotic, life was no longer as fulfilling as we had hoped."

"When *Raising Families* came into our community with their gospel of self-help it took us by surprise. Pastors had come to the envisioning and training sessions in great numbers. They had hoped that this was a new organisation that wanted to give stuff away. But the pastors cooperated and they began preaching this new gospel in the churches. To their amazement the churches received the vision wholeheartedly, and Church Action Groups were formed to drive the process."

"It was not long after this that that we were surprised when the pastors called all the CAGs to a meeting. At this meeting they informed us that they had taken a decision to stop the *RaFa* programme. When we asked them why, they told us that *RaFa* had not "come to the table" in giving the community any donations. The committee members were confused as for the first time we felt like we were achieving something for our community."

"We asked the pastors why they had passed this vision to us when they knew that *RaFa* had not promised anything from the start. They responded by saying that they now felt that no one could achieve this vision without material support. We were all saddened and articulated to the pastors that we had advanced so far with work that we wanted to continue with it, with the pastors' help. The meeting was cordial and the pastors decided to put it to the vote. I asked everyone that we pray before the vote and so we did. God performed a miracle that day, and the vote convincingly decided that we should continue with the programme. Some pastors chose not to continue but then changed their minds after more clarification by the Church Action Group. After 3 months the pastors also came and expressed their apologies for the misperception."

"Today all of the NGOs wanting to operate in our area have to go through our main committee, and their support goes to where it is needed first. Before any aid is given a deployment committee addresses the beneficiaries collectively on the importance of doing things for themselves, rather than just getting hand-outs. Many people have started to work their fields again. We now have a strong savings scheme and people are taking care of those in need. There is a gradual mind shift from dependency to a pride in utilising the community resources. Our committee household has refused to take anything from any NGOs except for agricultural inputs. We don't want their food and clothing hand-outs anymore. It was very difficult at first because our families fought with us. Now a new trend is emerging, people are embarrassed to take the free food and clothing. The chief has now decided no one is to accept any donation without a briefing from our committees! We believe that slowly our community is being restored back to where God wants us to be."

"Dignity has been restored to our families. I know that others have also been impacted. We have a different view of God now. Before this God was like Father Christmas to us. He had to give us things for us to be happy and worship Him. Now we just worship Him daily with thanksgiving for what He has given us from the beginning. Without *RaFa* coming God only knows where we would have ended up. Things were going downhill very fast. We thank God. He is now the centre of our community."

Burying the Demon of Impossibility

"Through this programme we have been empowered. Before the training we had an "impossibility mind-set", but now our thinking has changed. We actually even held a service to bury the demon of impossibility!" *CAG member from Gisanga, Rwanda.*

Education for the Price of a Coffee

"I have four children and through the savings and loans group I bought a hen. Selling the eggs helps me keep my children at school, providing uniforms and books. But the greatest benefit is the support of the group. I feel I have a new identity. It may only buy you a cup of tea in London, but one chicken sells for 2000 RWF (£1.80) and that helps me keep three children in junior school." *Community member in Mwali village, Nyamagana Parish, Rwanda.*

Questions for Group Discussion

- Where are the 'boundaries' between aid and development? When is aid appropriate, and when should aid give way to development?
- Which is the *quickest* and *easiest*; to give a fish, or to teach a person to fish?
- Which is the most *effective* and *sustainable*; to give a fish, or to teach a person to fish?
- Why do you think the church often settles merely for giving aid?
- How can we strengthen and transform our 'aid' initiatives (e.g. soup kitchens, clothing banks etc) so that they move along the spectrum from 'hand out' (aid) to 'hand up' (development)?
- What has to change in our *own* mindset before we can commit to 'teaching a man to fish'?

Study Five

Asset-Based Community Development

The value and importance of using local resources

What has God already put in my hand?

Over the years and across the world I have come across amazing, dynamic people, who have a wonderful vision as to how to bring effective Christ-like transformation to their communities. They have plans in place and are ready to go. "Our vision is for a rehab centre." "Our vision is to open a hospital."

But there is one problem. They are still on the starting line. They are like children sitting behind the wheel of their father's parked car. It's all 'brmm' and no movement. It's all theory. They are trying to steer a stationary object. All they need, they tell me, are funds; Samaritan's Purse funds.

I much prefer encountering people who are already using the limited resources they *have* got to get going on their journey of faith. They have a vision for a drug and alcohol rehab centre, so today they are feeding the homeless and building relationship with them. They have a vision for a community hospital, so today they are visiting the sick and praying with them in their homes.

They are learning lessons of faith and wisdom as they go. Jesus says to them, "Well done, good and faithful servants! You have been faithful with a few things; I will put you in charge of many things. Come and share your master's happiness!"

It's not that I'm blaming those who stay on the start line. In many ways, it is the western donors' capacity for dishing out money so randomly that has caused this 'hand-out mindset' to develop and, specifically in a Christian context, it's the ultimately unwise donations of rich and well-meaning believers that has even made the dubious expectation of an inundation of foreign funds a possibility.

In June 2009 I took a short-term team of volunteers to come alongside the church in northern Uganda, which was slowly recovering from the era of dreadful atrocities inflicted by the LRA rebel group in the 1990s. It was my first time in Uganda, and some amazing things happened around us as God brought salvation, healing and deliverance to many people.

But returning to Kampala from the South Sudanese border, we stopped to buy some food in Gulu (population 130,000), the city made famous by the 'Invisible Children' documentary film of 2006, and where at one time up to 15,000 children, known as 'night commuters', were fleeing into the city every evening for safety from the LRA.

I was amazed to see just how many international NGOs were still operating in the city, and my inner response surprised me. I felt *embarrassed*. Apparently at one time 500 organisations, catering for every possible aspect of human need, had a presence there. Hundreds remain there even now. In themselves, I'm sure they are doing some good, but these days, as I work more regularly in northern Uganda, I can also see for myself the damage that their presence has caused to the *work ethic* of the population. At one time the population was hard-working, but these days it is all too easy for people to seek hand-outs from these foreign agencies, some of whom (as discussed earlier) will even give what they call a 'sitting fee' to entice people to attend their trainings. Some families now even make their living purely by attending as many of these meetings as they can.

I have seen what I perceive to be the same mindset damage done in the Balkans where a very well respected pastor and good friend of mine was absolutely adamant that his church should be funded by the west for whatever programme or building project he felt prompted to initiate. "It is *your* responsibility" he told me, despite him having access to a wealth of foreign funds the likes of which my own church in the UK has never seen and is never likely to see.

I regularly see the same expectations in the former Soviet Union and other Eastern Bloc countries. Whilst in Ukraine, I encountered a pastor who angrily stood in a large public meeting and with clenched fists shouted at me and a handful of other western visitors, saying that we had all betrayed him by gradually bringing to an end the US-donated salary that he had been paid since 1990. Our most courteous hosts were very apologetic and embarrassed by his strong 'sense of entitlement', and tried to shut him up, but I felt it was a very interesting issue that, albeit maybe with a little more tact, was worthy of an airing. Churches with huge buildings designed by American architects, paid for by American Christians, built by a succession of American short term teams, and handed over to local but American-funded pastors, proved difficult to maintain when Western interest in the area became no longer trendy, and when global finances crashed in 2008. The visitors had spoken 'contract'. The hosts had heard 'covenant'. Belarus, Ukraine, Moldova, Russia, Croatia, Serbia, Romania. These are just some of the countries where I have witnessed this phenomenon personally.

But enough of the problem! It's what to do about it that matters most.

As discussed in the previous study ('The Aid and Development Spectrum'), there is clearly a time for the giving of aid. When the sheer survival of lives is critical, let us give relief, generously and without hesitation. It's just that many of us don't know when to stop, or rather to move on from this emergency strategy into something more sustainable and wholesome. I believe that even emergency aid needs to be given with our eyes wide open to the next stages, i.e. those of recovery and development.

In a very stretching five weeks I spent in Sri Lanka immediately after the 2004 South East Asian Tsunami, one responsibility I was tasked with was to decide exactly where to position a new housing complex which was to be urgently built in an area devastated by the tidal wave. Although I had the authority of the funders and local authorities to make this decision, and despite the urgency and debilitating trauma still being experienced by the beneficiaries, my greatest concern was to somehow understand the will of the people regarding this major decision and its long-lasting implications. As will be discussed in the next study ('Local Ownership'), it is not only local people's knowledge that we need, but their dignity, their self-worth and their sense of responsibility that are also very much at stake.

Raising Families is an 'asset based' programme. What this means is that rather than handing out external resources, we work on the basis of equipping people to see what they *already* have (be it time, land, skills, access etc), what to do with what they have, and how to do it. This is at the core of all our work. Later I'll outline how this works out in practice, but firstly, let's look into the scriptures.

The Biblical Rationale

<u>What do you have in your hand?</u>

Moses was having an interesting day. It was one he wouldn't forget in a hurry. It started with a burning bush, and continued with an intense conversation with the God of Abraham, of Isaac and of Jacob. He wasn't sure how these heroes of old had responded to such encounters, but for himself, Moses was finding it difficult to believe what he was hearing. God wanted him to spearhead the exodus of His people from Egypt. Moses afforded himself the luxury of asking a few simple questions, such as "Who am I that I should do this?", "Just suppose I do go, what shall I say?", and "What if they don't believe me?" It's God's answer to Moses third question that is significant for us here. The Lord said to him, *"What is that in your hand?"* (Exodus 4:2 NIV).

"A staff" Moses replied.

The Lord said, "Throw it on the ground". Moses obeyed and it became a snake, so Moses legged it. But God called him back and told him to take the snake by the tail. As he did so, it turned back into a staff in his hand. With this and other miracles, Moses was to convince his listeners that he was called by God and was to be believed and trusted.

You might recall a similar question being asked in 2 Kings 4:2 (NIV). This time it was Elisha, speaking with the distraught widow of a prophet who was about to have to forfeit her two sons as slaves to a creditor. *"How can I help you?"* asked Elisha. *"Tell me, what do you have in your house?"*

All she had was a little olive oil, but Elisha encouraged the woman to collect as many empty jars as she could from her neighbours, then to shut the door and pour oil into all the jars. This she did, and the oil kept flowing until no other jar could be found. Selling the oil, she paid off her debts.

Exodus 4:2 – What do you have in your hand? 2 Kings 4:2 – What do you have in your house?

We can also be inspired by Shamgar who, we are told in Judges 3:31, struck down six hundred Philistines with a stick (or an ox-goad). He did what he could, where he was and with what he had.

Benaiah had a similar story to tell in 2 Samuel 23:20-21. He struck down a huge Egyptian. Although the Egyptian had a spear in his hand, Benaiah went against him with a club.

Jesus employed the same principle when training His disciples in John 6:8-11 (NIV). Faced with a great crowd of friendly but hungry people coming towards them, Jesus said to Philip, *"Where shall we buy bread for these people to eat?"* Philip hadn't a clue, seeing only the need in front of him. It was Andrew, Simon Peter's brother, who spoke up, albeit sounding a bit pathetic. *"Here is a boy with five small barley loaves and two small fish, but how far will they go among so many?"* You know the story. Five thousand men ate as much as they wanted that day, and there were twelve baskets left over.

Fast forward to the early church (Acts 3:1-10), and we find Peter and John on their way to pray at the temple, where they were accosted by a lame man asking for money. Peter replied, *"Silver and gold I do not have, but what I do have I give to you. In the name of Jesus Christ of Nazareth, walk."* (Acts 3:6 NIV).

What have you got in your hand? What do you have in your house? Not only did God teach these people how to take their focus off the problem and onto what they already had (i.e. off their needs and onto their assets) in order to meet their own security, their own survival, and to pay off their own debts, but (particularly in the New Testament) we see how these somewhat limited assets were to be shared with others, so as to be a blessing to the hungry and to the lame.

So what has God put into your hand? What has He put in mine? To my shame, I think there are many times I've effectively said no to God, or whinged, or run away, or given up, or stayed silent, because...

- I lacked confidence (like Moses)
- I could not see any answers to my predicament (like the prophet's wife)

- It seemed that my opponent was too strong (*un*like Shamgar or Benaiah)
- I wanted to keep my resources for myself (*un*like the boy with the loaves and fish)
- I missed the God-given moment due to being dull of faith (*un*like Peter)

Finally, here are two more scriptures that encourage us to use the *weak* things and the *few* things that we already have for the glory of God.

"But he said to me, 'My grace is sufficient for you, for my power is made perfect in weakness.' Therefore I will boast all the more gladly about my weaknesses, so that Christ's power may rest on me." (2 Corinthians 12:9 NIV).

"His master replied, 'Well done, good and faithful servant! You have been faithful with a few things; I will put you in charge of many things. Come and share your master's happiness!" (Matthew 25:21 NIV).

The Raising Families Context

We often refer to these and other similar scriptures when encouraging the churches we work with to see what they already have, and to see the *potential* of what they already have. We then typically teach each church how to complete not only a needs analysis but also an assets analysis.

Our national coordinators regularly tell me how revolutionary this process is, and what a joy it is to behold. Communities start by telling them how desperately poor they are. All they see are their needs. When asked by our facilitators what they have, they all say they have nothing, and that they are in the poorest segment of society. Little by little my colleagues help them to see that despite their difficulties and limitations, it is not strictly true to say they have nothing. The communities begin to see that they have all sorts of resources which, if used well and in cooperation with one another, can have a significant impact on their families' lives and the well-being of their community. Some have land and some have time. Others have knowledge, and others still have practical skills. And some have *access*, e.g. to important people who can get things changed. "My brother works in the education department." "My son's best friend is the son of the regional health director's gardener." Access is a precious and empowering commodity.

Our *Raising Families* budget for each country's programme reflects our commitment to ABCD (Asset-Based Community Development). In all but one of our programmes around the world, 100% of the budget is spent on trainer costs. In this way the programme not only offers dignity and self-worth to the local community, but it also represents extraordinary value for money to our donors.[8]

One story I love came from a church in Swaziland[9]. They wanted to express their gratitude to God for Him opening their eyes to what they already had, and had a solid testimony of using those resources, rather than gifts and donations, to lift themselves out of ultra-poverty. *"Raising Families* came and promised us nothing,"* they reported. "And that's exactly what they delivered!" It made me chuckle, but actually it's a great quote! And here are some more.

Testimonies from Raising Families Practitioners

Poverty no longer outside of our control

---

[8] The one exception to this is our *Raising Families* programme in Kyrgyzstan, where one line of the budget is for small sub grants that are selectively and occasionally used to provide capital as a 'hand up' for enterprises such as a dairy farm, a disabled children's day centre, and a small sowing factory; community-based initiatives which in this lower-middle income country with cold-climate infrastructure would clearly be beyond the reach of the families we are working with.

[9] On 19 April 2018, King Mswati III announced that Swaziland had officially changed its name to Eswatini. As all the stories and illustrations I've used from this nation are from before April 2018, I have chosen to refer to the country as Swaziland throughout this book.

"I tell our people, 'Don't talk to me about poverty. Fundamentally it's not material. It's about relationships, attitudes to work, things like that. So don't talk to me about poverty as though it's outside our control. It's not. There are things we can do about it ourselves.'" *Raising Families Coordinator, Rwanda.*

Saving for a rainy day

The Church Action Group in near Siphofaneni, Swaziland, undertook a community asset review. Nearby was the site of a failed EU-funded garden project, which despite the undergrowth and obvious signs of abandonment, still had a dam, and fencing around its 2.5 hectare site. The result of the community's asset review pointed quite naturally to the restoration of this site, only this time with a sustainable community ownership model which the CAG was confident could be achieved through *Raising Families*. Despite the drought, which had seriously slowed their efforts, Flora Ntombi and her small group of ageing ladies are now ready to harvest their first crop of Cayenne peppers. All they were waiting for was the distributor's truck to be mended. Cayenne peppers are apparently good for treating TB and other sicknesses. They were also growing drought resistant Jalapeno and Habanero peppers and Moringa trees. The garden is totally organic. They use cow and chicken manure, vegetable mulch, non-chemical insecticides, and grow plants that alkaline the soil. "Because the pump has broken down, we are only limited by how much water we can carry up from the dam on our heads. We also have a thriving savings and loans scheme." said Flora. And then, without any hint of irony in this drought-parched landscape she added, "We're saving for a rainy day."

When life gives you lemons

Emelienne[10] knew the sour taste of poverty. Her small piece of land in Rwanda could barely provide enough food for her family, let alone enough to sell so that she might send her children to school. Everything changed when her local church introduced her to the *Raising Families* programme.

To Emelienne God had given two lemon trees, though locked into despair over her otherwise barren land, Emelienne had never realised the potential of what was right in front of her. With the help of her Church Action Group, which she met and prayed with regularly, she was encouraged to harvest and sell a first crop of lemons. She raised a healthy £5.00. Through the CAG savings group she was then able to borrow a little money, enough to buy lemon tree seedlings and grow a further 22 lemon trees. As she squeezed an income from the lemons she was able to buy banana plants and livestock, and now her children go to school and the family have vital health care insurance.

---

[10] Emelienne and her story were the stars of the *Raising Families* video used by Spring Harvest as their main-stage mission of choice at each of their 2017 events. The four minute video can be downloaded from my website: http://www.cuttingacross.com/videos.html

Emelienne is also known for giving away lemon saplings and helping others in her community. Her story spread and now people from other neighbouring communities come to learn more of how Church Action Groups can help them.

The church has come down to the people, and the people have come up to God

With my colleagues from the Province of the Anglican Church of Rwanda, I visited Wingugu village in Nkumbure Parish. Alexi introduced himself as one of the Church Action Group leaders.

"For me light dawned when I read 2 Kings 4:1-7." He told us. "Elisha asked the widow, 'What do you have in your house?' And God provided through what she had, not what she hadn't got. So we counted up our assets, and together we said 'No!' to poverty. I constructed a vegetable garden and then taught my neighbours how to do the same. We encourage all our families to invest into health care insurance. All our children are now studying. We visit the sick, but we never go empty handed."

"Now that the church has come down to the people, the people have come up to God. And now our tiny village is even receiving a visit from the Province, and even this *mzungu* has come all the way from Europe to visit us!"

This was greeted with almost incredulous laughter, joy and applause. And at this point, extraordinarily, we were presented with a gift of two huge sacks of locally grown potatoes.

My colleague from the Province stood to thank the village for their gift. "When a car from the diocese used to turn up in the village," he said, "people would always run after it to see what was going to be given to them. Now we come and you give *us* gifts! This is transformation! Praise God!"

Raising funds from what we already have

Empunzweni community is a very poor area in Swaziland that has suffered greatly from drought and serious health related challenges. This area has also been the scene of a chieftaincy rivalry that has lasted for 12 years, and this had adversely affected the community's livelihoods. The people have always believed that they are cursed because nothing seems to prosper or develop. The church had tried to bring encouragement and hope but the message was not being well received.

When *Raising Families* began envisioning in the community, Pastor Paul Kunene's church caught the vision. They had been working hard at applying what they learned. It was not easy because people believed that such a paradigm shift was not possible in their community. It took a very long time for Greater Harvest Church to form a solid Church Action Group. People would volunteer and fall away again and again. The church only had about 52 members and most of them deemed themselves as vulnerable and destitute.

After a long struggle Pastor Paul prayed and asked God to provide him with a strong leader that would help form a permanent committee. His prayer were answered when Thuli stepped up and volunteered. Thuli (aged 78) had a different spirit. She began by telling her colleagues that she will be the first to demonstrate that it is possible to make a difference. Thuli had a collection of donated clothing that was being distributed by other organisations that regularly came into her community. She had told her friends that she was tired of hoarding things. She feared that she might die and have to leave something for her children. She shared how God had spoken to her and showed her that He was a God that replenishes every act of kindness and generosity. She shared with the church one day the story in the bible (2 King 4:1-7) of the poor widow that was about to lose her sons to her creditors. The prophet Elisha asked her "what she had in her house". She remembered that she had hoarded so much it filled 3 large trunk boxes. She also remembered how God through Elisha had told the widow to find every available vessel she could.

So one Saturday she took all the donated clothes and shoes to the neighbouring community's market day. She sold everything at a very low price and was pleasantly surprised to see that the people bought everything. On Sunday she shared her story and handed the money to the pastor to help buy food for 3 poor families. Everyone was amazed including the pastor. The following Sunday people just began to bring donated items for Thuli to sell at the next market day. This happened Sunday after Sunday until Thuli challenged others to help her. 7 woman volunteered and 22 poor families are being supported to this day from items that keep getting donated in the community.

When other churches heard about what Greater Harvest Church was doing they began to copy what was being done. The pastors from the 3 active churches suggested that the committees work together for greater impact. They then decided to form their own market day. To Thuli's amazement it was a modest success, and so they did not give up. Today the new market day happens every second Saturday and sales are reasonably good. Donated items have increased and literally flooded the churches, and the community is happy to buy at the market. Thuli remarks, "Only God can do such a thing. It does not make sense, but the more we give to the churches, the more things organisations bring. It blesses me to see that so many people have been empowered, and even if the donations were to stop we will succeed; we have enough resources now. Somehow people wait for market day to buy the very things that have been donated. It seems strange but it has given people a sense of self-worth and pride and a reason for fellowship. Our church has grown and so have the others."

Questions for Group Discussion

- Why do you think many donors find it less attractive to invest into 'invisibles' such as training and behaviour change, preferring instead to give items such as chickens, goats, church buildings and second hand clothes?
- Discuss why it would seem that donors get more fulfilment in buying something 'instant and visual', whether or not donor fulfilment should really matter, and how we can help one another to lower our demand for personal fulfilment in our giving.
- So what has God put into our hand? List the resources that we in this room already have, and how they could benefit our community.
- When have I said 'no' to God, or whinged, or ran away, or given up, or stayed silent, because...
  - I lacked confidence (like Moses)?
  - It seems that my opponent was too strong (unlike Shamgar or Benaiah)?
  - I could not see any answers to my predicament (like the prophet's wife)?
  - I wanted to keep my resources for myself (unlike the boy with the loaves and fish)?
  - I missed the God-given moment due to being dull of faith (unlike Peter)?
- What initial steps would you take as a church if you were to undertake a needs and assets survey in your community?

Study Six

Local Ownership

Regarding the programme as their own

People Cannot Be Developed

The often-used expression, "A poor thing, but mine own" is a misquote from Shakespeare when, in *"As You Like It"* (Act 5, Scene 4, Page 4), Touchstone basically says of his girlfriend Audrey, "She ain't much to look at, but at least she's mine!" Rather than us dwelling on the limited beauty of Audrey, it's the second part of this quote that I want to bring into focus here. In this chapter we will discuss the immense importance and value, even the necessity, of local ownership.

In Britain, we might say 'What's the big deal?', and could be tempted, even unwittingly, to wrest ownership away from the roots on the justification that we, the outsider with a wonderful worldview, know better. We need long memories if we are to recall the last invasion of our mainland shores, and when the 'local ownership' of our own destiny was under threat. Debate rages as to when this was. Some say 'the last successful invasion of Britain' was in 1688, when William III landed an army in Devon. Others tell us 'the last opposed invasion of Britain' was at Landguard Fort, Felixstowe, the site of the 1667 first land battle of The Duke of York and Albany's Marines in the second Anglo-Dutch war. Spinning it slightly differently still, others might argue that 'the last time Britain was invaded by a foreign power'[11] was the Battle of Fishguard in February 1797, when Revolutionary France landed hostile troops on our shores and went a full two days before unconditionally surrendering.

All this to say that for ethnic British citizens, we as a people really cannot intrinsically understand what it means or how it *feels* to be dominated, oppressed or controlled. It has 'always' been this way, at least for 220 years. Our parliament is among the oldest in the world, and when the EU started tampering with a few of our practices over the past generation or two, we fairly soon said 'no more' to them as well. But for nations that have been invaded, dominated and oppressed, pushed and poked, colonised and controlled, attacked and abused, sometimes every few years and by different external forces, a cautious and defensive attitude almost inevitably becomes a part of the culture and psyche of its people, its laws, its approach to international relationships etc. Ownership, and the opportunity to become the architects of one's own destiny, become very precious commodities indeed.

---

[11] https://www.thetimes.co.uk/article/the-last-invasion-of-britain-wl0r3s9l9

In the same spirit of assumed control, Christians have often offered a gospel on the basis of the pointing finger that says, '*We* know what *you* need', or '*We* know how *you* need to live', and have not listened deeply enough to the heart and the felt needs of those we seek to support. We have not thought twice about their dignity and self-worth, but have come with a dominator mentality. Mercy has not always triumphed over judgement.

And it is all too easy for NGOs to ride into town in their white Land Cruisers, harbouring the same attitudes and thoughtless assumptions. Much has been discussed about this power imbalance, and its negative effects, but there is still plenty of room for us to give more thought to how to be simply ready to offer what we have, when invited, and in a way that results in other people's growth in understanding, knowledge, education, health etc, all within a context of their own dignity and self-worth.

I was almost an adult before I gained any concept at all of the need for a roof over my head. It was just there. It was for someone else to worry about; to pay for; to mend. I had totally taken it for granted, until at the age of 17 I suddenly had to find that very same commodity for myself.

And another 'penny dropped' when I moved from renting a property to purchasing one, albeit with a hefty mortgage. Suddenly I took an interest. I enquired. I cared. I cherished. I planned. I defended. I mowed and I sowed. I owned.

The same thing happened as my own son went from borrowing his mother's car (a loan which resulted in many bashes and scrapes, and very little cleaning or maintenance or refuelling) to purchasing his own (which miraculously resulted in an immediate ritual of daily washing, grooming, preening, polishing, and the purchasing of fancy accessories etc).

Local ownership. It's healthy. It matures us all. It opens our eyes, it maintains our dignity, it establishes our self-worth, and it fosters responsibility. And, although the world sees *in*dependence as the goal of life, the gospel actually aims for inter-dependence (Romans 12:3-8). We need one another, and we each need to play our part.

The world of development is full of stories about nameless NGO workers who arrive in a village, see a need, and seek to meet that need by delivering an asset, such as a water pump or well. Typically the story goes like this. The villagers gather round to watch while the foreigners firstly plan its location, and then sweat and toil over building it. And, because a free lunch is offered by the NGO, the villagers even attend training on how the pump should be used. Everyone celebrates and the NGO drives off into the sunset. One of the NGO workers returns to the village a couple of years later to find it broken, rusting, and with weeds growing up around it. He is shocked and disappointed and asks, "Why aren't you using it?" The villages just shrug their shoulders.

"Well it broke. It isn't ours. It's yours. We just assumed you would come back one day and mend your pump."

"People cannot be developed," said Julius Nyerere, the former President of Tanzania. "They can only develop themselves."

An Exercise

To work towards a healthier alternative, my colleagues have sometimes used the following exercise with the communities they serve.

With a group of 8-10 people, ask one to step temporarily out of sight and earshot. Then ask the remaining group members to hold hands in a circle, and then to tangle themselves up whilst still holding hands, e.g. by ducking under the arms of another two people etc. Then invite the 'outsider' back, and task them with untangling the group.

At the end of this exercise, ask the same group of 8-10 people *all* to hold hands in a circle again, and to all tangle themselves up whilst still holding hands. Then task them with untangling themselves.

Sit the group down and ask them what they observed, compare and contrast these two scenarios.

Typical responses might include:

Scenario A

It was obvious that the outsider doesn't know or understand how the muddle came about.

However, maybe the outsider was better positioned to observe things from a more objective viewpoint.

Leadership and control was established quickly, but in the end it wasn't very effective leadership either in terms of building morale or in getting the job done.

The outsider could not feel the pain of the group, and we were worried that they could get discouraged and give up, leaving the group in a worse muddle than they were in at the start.

Scenario B

The group members were more likely to recall who did what (and in which order) to get themselves into the muddle, and therefore had better solutions for resolving the problem.

Leadership took time to get established, initially causing everyone to talk rather than to listen, which resulted in some random and isolated actions, debate and argument, but before too long natural, recognised and respected leadership emerged.

The problem caused suffering to the group personally, so initiative and motivation to resolve things was always more likely to happen.

Much more camaraderie was built during the untangling process, and a greater sense of achievement and fulfilment came when the problem was eventually solved together.

The Biblical Rationale

There is something really fundamental about man being built for ownership and responsibility, and for working hard with the resources he's been given. And it's been there for a very long time.

"God said, 'Let us make mankind in our image, in our likeness, so that they may rule over the fish in the sea and the birds in the sky, over the livestock and all the wild animals, and over all the creatures that move along the ground.'

So God created mankind in his own image, in the image of God he created them; male and female he created them.

God blessed them and said to them, 'Be fruitful and increase in number; fill the earth and subdue it. Rule over the fish in the sea and the birds in the sky and over every living creature that moves on the ground.'" (Genesis 1:26-28 NIV)

Nehemiah is a great example of someone who by prayer (1:5-11), faith in God (2:20), and with vision, planning and determination, took ownership and responsibility for his own community. He saw the trouble its people were in (2:17) and, despite heartache (1:4), restrictions, fears (2:2), long hours (2:13), mocking opposition and accusation (2:19), hardships and setbacks, Nehemiah believed that the God of heaven would give them success (2:20). He made special efforts to defend the poor against injustice (5:1-13), he warmly welcomed foreigners (5:17), he appointed Godly leaders (7:1-2), and he did everything he could to ensure the people were restored to a relationship with God (8-13). What an amazing story of community transformation, initiated and executed without 'outside' help!

Similarly, when Jesus told the parable of the talents, we see Him praising the servants who didn't wait for the experts to arrive, but who instead rolled up their sleeves and made something happen with the resources and responsibilities that had been given to them. *"Well done, good and faithful servants!"* their master said upon his return (Matthew 25:21, 23 NIV). But He wasn't nearly so encouraging to the work-shy servant who did nothing with what he'd been given (Matthew 25:26-30). In contrast to the initiatives the other two servants had shown, this chap dug a hole for himself, buried the assets, fostered negative thoughts about authority, made excuses, blamed others and, as a result, lost everything he had.

Proverbs makes regular mention of the wisdom and particularly of the dignity that comes from making things happen locally. The reader of Proverbs 3.21 (NIV) is encouraged not to *"let wisdom* and understanding out of your sight," and to *"preserve sound judgment and discretion."* And the *"wife of noble character"* in Proverbs 31 *"is clothed with strength and dignity; she can laugh at the days to come"* (v25 NIV).

All these scriptures are great exhortations and encouragements to the local community, but what does the bible say to those who are visitors, guests, or external implementers? There is plenty of encouragement in the scriptures as to how to behave when we are the 'aliens in the land'. We are not only to graciously receive the hospitality of our hosts, but also to act legally, responsibly, humbly, honourably and with respectful regard to local culture and customs. We are to come not with ideas of dominance or a rigid agenda, but with blessing. *"When you first enter a house, first say, 'Peace to this house'"* (Luke 10:5 NIV).

Anyone who anticipates being given authority in a foreign land should therefore walk very carefully and with humility. When Paul met with the Ephesian elders for a final time, he reviewed how he had approached his previous visits to Ephesus (Acts 20:17-27 NIV). *"I served the Lord with great humility and with tears...for I have not hesitated to proclaim to you the whole will of God."* Similarly he reminded the Corinthians that his visits there were *"in purity, understanding, patience and kindness, in the Holy Spirit and in sincere love"*, concluding, *"We... opened wide our hearts to you"* (2 Corinthians 6:6, 11 NIV).

But coming as He did from heaven to live on earth, surely Jesus, Son of God, was an exception to this rule? Not at all! He said to His disciples, *"You know that the rulers of the Gentiles lord it over them, and their high officials exercise authority over them. Not so with you. Instead, whoever wants to become great among you must be your servant, and whoever wants to be first must be your slave – just as the Son of Man did not come to be served, but to serve, and to give his life as a ransom for many"* (Matthew 20:25-28 NIV).

Let me describe how I see this working out in a *Raising Families* context.

The Raising Families Context

"We've had a mind-set change from missionary times. They'd come to fix our lives, and so we couldn't ever see our resources and our potential. Now we've seen them, we realise we are rich! This has come just at the right time."
Bishop of Kigali Diocese, Rwanda.

As someone wise once said, good mission is seeing where God is already at work, and joining in. When offering *Raising Families* programmes, Samaritan's Purse UK recognises that it stands on holy ground. We are not apostles, as though the foreign funders of programmes possess some God-given right to speak with authority into the state of each local church they happen to meet. Instead, we are merely supporters, enablers, facilitators, where invited, always honouring the local church as God's main agent of the Kingdom of God on earth, and sincerely rejoicing over the opportunities we are given to serve alongside them. *"The earth is the Lord's and everything in it, the world, and all who live in it"* (Psalm 24:1 NIV). Like Abraham, we are looking forward to the city (or the church, or the village) *"with foundations, whose architect and builder is God"* (Hebrews 11:10 NIV).

So from the outset we will only go to countries where we have been invited, and where we have had the time to build up a relationship of trust and true partnership with like-minded agencies. Likewise, our national partners will only go to churches where they have been welcomed, and local churches will only work with communities and families where they have been invited. In that way, we can say with Paul, *"I thank my God every time I remember you. In all my prayers for all of you, I always pray with joy because of your* partnership *in the gospel from the first day until now, being confident of this, that he who began a good work in you will carry it on to completion until the day of Christ Jesus"* (Philippians 1:3-6 NIV).

We do acknowledge that this *'partnership in the gospel'* clearly requires all partners and contributors to become active stakeholders, each having roles and responsibilities, and undertaking them in a spirit of joint two-way cooperation. An example of where the local partner responds to the needs of the *donor* agency (in this case Samaritan's Purse) is where our donors want to know that they are getting value for money, and so we ask our partners and the churches and families they are working with to undertake monitoring and evaluation processes, and provide us with the results.

But whilst having a recognisable global model and rationale, and fairly standard and contractual reporting requirements, the *Raising Families* programme is tailored to be appropriate to each social, economic and regulatory culture and context that we work in. For example; HIV awareness training in Swaziland, conflict recovery in Rwanda and NW Uganda, and bridge-building in a post-Soviet Islamic-majority context in Central Asia. Also, each local church is encouraged to provide an appropriate offering of training and services to the families they serve through completing initial family-specific assets- and needs-assessments. In this way the programme content and emphasis is locally owned, and each family becomes the designer of their own destiny.

"People used to come to the Archbishop and ask for funds and help. We would ask them if they had spoken with their pastor. "They can't help us." Had they spoken with their Bishop? "They can't help us either". So we would get involved, but there was always a missing link. I longed for the day when parishes would see this sort of thing as their own issue. Then Samaritan's Purse came in 2008, and told us they wanted to help empower local churches to be the hands and feet of Jesus in their communities. I thought, "How do you empower the local church?" But slowly we learned. They took me to Kenya to look at other models. I became very much eager to learn. I confess that I had never seen an initiative that encouraged the local church to empower themselves. Now the Bishops are so excited. These days' people *want* to report back to us before they are asked to. In the past we took money from donors to build wells and suchlike. So the churches learned to expect it. Now we have fully shifted from that mentality – there is zero financial investment from outside. We challenge churches to learn that God is not mean. He's put the resources in the community that He wants us to use. Jesus said that the blind will see, and so they do. They now see what they already have and they use it. We have to be patient, but actually people have caught the vision quickly, and the moment people see what Jesus sees, they put their faith in action and share their love with their neighbours."

National Coordinator, Raising Families Programme, Rwanda.

Testimony from a Raising Families Practitioner

Zamo Hlanze is a *Raising Families* Church Action Group leader from Zimpofu in Swaziland. Here is her story:

"Ours has always been a very poor but motivated community. There have been many initiatives and projects led by a large NGO and the government. Most of the projects have failed because the people had no real revelation and 'buy in', as the projects were very prescriptive in nature. Two agencies came and just began to give away free food, building material, agricultural inputs and fencing etc. When BBI *(Samaritan's Purse's partner in Swaziland)* arrived in the community most of these projects were already defunct and the tangible materials and structure had been vandalised or stolen."

"The reason for this was the fact that no one felt responsible for what they had been asked to do. No one contributed to any of the work other than in labour only. As soon as the agencies left, slowly but surely all the work just fell apart. The community had gotten used to the outside assistance and now depended too much on the donors. As a result of this intervention by these two main agents and others there was a tendency to sit back and wait for the next project to be introduced into the community."

"When BBI came into our community we believed that they would do just as the other NGOs and government had done. So we listened to what they said and we just waited for the trucks to start delivering material, seeds and food as before. To our amazement and disappointment after a few months they stuck to their vision of saying that they would not give us anything because we already had everything. This was a new concept to us and it reminded us of how we were slowly progressing before the NGOs and government came to our community."

"BBI talked to us and taught us how to recognise what we already have in our communities. It took a lot of convincing that they were not going to give us anything. We waited and waited until we were convinced that nothing was going to be forthcoming. It was at this point that the pastors got together and questioned BBI on their motives. It was decided that a community meeting be called for BBI to explain themselves more clearly. It was during that meeting that the BBI staff used the bible to describe to us what God had already done for us, and what He had already given us. During this meeting I saw two elderly women weeping quietly as if they had deep regret. One of them later stood up to addressed the gathering. She shared how she had been touched by the envisioning, and how it reminded her of the better life they had before donors came into their communities and disturbed their organic development. She also asked where their projects were now and what had become of them. The people seemed embarrassed and ashamed. This is when we decided that we were willing to work with BBI. It's a pity as it took us more than 4 months to catch this vision."

"As a result of all the work and training done by the BBI staff, we began deciding on projects that we had wanted to do. BBI taught us to consider the destitute and most vulnerable, but we chose to develop what we could first, and then reach-out to the greater community. Our committees decided on an ambitious project of building our community a small warehouse for processing and selling our wares and produce. Our churches took a special offering for this work and every household that could contributed money. It was not easy because some of the people had no money. I was one of those that found it very difficult to pay the £16 that everyone had committed to every month. But because we had all caught the vision we persevered."

"However when we had almost finished this long project a cyclone came and damaged the building. We were so discouraged, as we had spent a lot of money and resources putting up this structure. Our dream was shattered!"

"After a lot of prayer and encouragement from the BBI staff we decided to continue selling our wares in the open along the roadside to the bus passengers and passers-by. Business was reasonable and very quickly we made some money so we were able to repair the damaged building. Now the building is almost complete. We have already started using the building to hold meetings and combined church services and community prayer meetings. People from other communities come and join us in worship and prayer and many lives have been touched. We had not envisaged the spiritual impact that this building would have. The building has become our community centre where people come to meet, worship, pray and sell their wares. Our committee has decided to support 50 orphaned children, by feeding them and buying clothing and school uniforms for them. So many people have been helped as a result of all this work."

"We have many plans for our centre, but during the day it will be our market and processing point for our community," says Zamo.

"I had lost my sense of a sound self-esteem, because I would often find myself literally begging from people whom I perceived as 'wealthy' that came visiting in our community. I would always plead poverty and I considered myself destitute and poor before. Now I am proud of myself and my community, now I want to take care of it and develop it. I love my church because it has grown and the pastor has now become a different man. He is so anointed and effective now."

"My life has changed because I am now able to afford school fees for my own children and for others too. My dignity is restored and now we relate to each other differently and with some authority. Our spiritual lives have improved so much that people are committing themselves to Christ. And more than 220 orphans are being assisted in one way or another."

Questions for Group Discussion

- Compare and contrast the feelings of attachment and depth of ownership that people in your group have towards the property they live in, whether it be shared, rented, owned etc.
- When and in what situations have group members felt most controlled or dictated to by other 'outsiders'?
- It has been suggested that another appropriate way to express 'poverty' is 'powerlessness'. Share your thoughts together on the meaning of powerlessness, using practical illustrations where possible.
- How much of what we offer as a church is controlled by our own assumptions of what the community needs?

- What are the long term impacts of a programme, an attitude or an approach which is imposed on others, without adequate consultation or ownership?
- In what practical ways can we as a church begin to address this need for local ownership?

Study Seven

The Focus on Families

Why families are the core building block

There are a number of agencies that provide similar services to Raising Families. Collectively, they tend to be called Church and Community Mobilisers, or similar such names. Some focus on children, others on communities as a whole, and others still on sectors such as livelihoods or health. This study looks at why Raising Families focuses on the family unit.

Home Sweet Home

I've travelled a lot over the last thirty years. Ninety-nine different countries at the last count. So people often ask me which my favourite country is. Others phrase it a little differently. "Where's your favourite destination?" There's only one answer to this, and that's 'Home'. For one who is such a traveller, I always love putting the key into the lock of my own front door. If travel were ever to become an escape from the reality and responsibilities of home, then something would be very wrong.

I love the same sort of household that Jesus loved – the one where Martha, Lazarus and Mary lived. We read about it in John chapter 12, when Jesus was invited to dinner in celebration of the fact that he'd just raised Lazarus from the dead.

It was actually a very attractive environment – really good friends celebrating an amazing event together. A bit like the parties 'The Beautiful People' apparently go to, and which much of the world jealously watches on music videos and Martini adverts. A place to which (we are told) we would all like to be invited, accepted, gathered up; included.

Imagine Martha. Sleeves rolled up, she's in the kitchen. OK, she can get a bit wound up at times, and she remembers with a coy smile the day that Jesus had a word with her about that. She'd listened well, and His word had been transforming, and as a result, tonight she's in her element. She's been working away all day in order to prepare the very best food for the dinner party, and she's loved every minute of it. She would really like to be mingling with the guests as well, but tonight Martha knows she has a job to do and, despite the sacrifice, and refusing to feel left out, she joyfully accepts the responsibility. She brings out another plate of food and places it near to Lazarus, who is reclining at table with Jesus.

Lazarus gets up, takes the plate, and begins meandering around the room, networking, relating; oozing with radiant joy out of his massive gratitude for the miracle of life. At the same time he listens attentively to his guests, expressing genuine interest in the comparatively mundane anecdotes of their week. "More orange squash, anyone? Quiche? Cheesy dips?" (Well, it is a *Christian* party remember!).

Imagine a latecomer, tumbling in straight from work, hastily removing his coat, rushing straight into a deep conversation with someone, and absent-mindedly grabbing a fist full of food from the passing tray. "Oh cheers mate." Then he looks up in mid-sentence, sees Lazarus and, utterly stunned, stops in his tracks. "Blimey, Lazarus, I thought you were dead? Hey mate, I'm sorry I didn't make the funeral. I was *so* busy. You know how it is. I'd just bought a field and had to go and view it. I'd just bought five yoke of oxen and had to take them for a test drive. Oh, and I'd just got married as well. Anyway, how did it go? Although I suppose you wouldn't really know, would you? Err, feeling any better now?"

Precisely at this moment an incident takes place that radically transforms the evening. Mary, spontaneously, shockingly prepared to break with the cultural norm for the greater good, takes half a litre of pure nard[12] costing the equivalent of a year's wages, elegantly kneels down, and simply pours it over Jesus' feet. The buzz of conversation plummets like a stone and, in the deafening silence, the whole building instantly fills with the

---

[12] A perennial aromatic plant of the valerian family. Flowers: pinkish-purple. Native to: Himalayan range. Latin name *Nardostachys jatamansi*

amazing fragrance of the perfume. You could cut the atmosphere with a knife.

Undeterred, unhurried, and with *such* grace, Mary then loosens her hair, stoops even further down, and wipes Jesus' feet - with her hair! Guests involuntarily place their hands over their mouths and faces, totally shocked and embarrassed. They exchange panicked glances at one another, wondering just what on earth has got into the normally sweet and modest Mary. These were the flagrant and suggestive actions of a prostitute, and yet she seemed totally oblivious of the fuss she was causing. There was nowhere for the guests to hide. This was just so *wrong*, so un-cool, such a cultural faux pas, *so* embarrassing.

It was Judas who broke the silence. He was *angry*. "*Why*? Why wasn't this perfume sold, and the money given to the poor?" And with deep frustrated rage, he clasped his hands together behind his neck and shouted into the sky, "It was worth *a year's wages!*"

He didn't say this because he cared about the poor but because he was a thief; as keeper of the money bag, he used to help himself to what was put into it.

Every one of the disciples had had their suspicions about Judas, but at this moment in time that just didn't matter. They weren't thieves, but on this occasion they actually all completely *agreed* with Judas. There wasn't an Englishman among them, but even these flamboyant Middle Eastern guys were just too cultured, too conventional, too ordered, too functional even to *dream* of accepting that such a thing could be happening right before their eyes.

Because she was in the kitchen, Martha didn't actually witness the incident. But she clearly sensed the sudden change of atmosphere, and came through to see why the strong aroma. And Lazarus? Well he was just happy to be alive. He thought his younger sister's gift was just brilliant. His head buzzed with praise, joy, laughter, awe. But of their guests, no one could even *begin* to cope with this ridiculous, overwhelmingly lavish act of celebratory worship that Mary had innocently poured out onto the Son of God.

No one, that is, except Jesus.

There had been no hint of embarrassment from Him. In fact at that moment He decided that in the following days *He* would wash His *disciples'* feet, knowing full well that once more they would react all over the place. He could just imagine it. "You'll *never* wash my feet!" But here, tonight, at the dinner given in His honour, He comfortably received exactly this same treatment. It just didn't matter that this was usually an act of extreme sensuality, or that the guests, to a man, had just been blasted further outside their comfort zone than they'd ever been before. Jesus relaxed, Jesus received, Jesus accepted, Jesus enjoyed. And Jesus replied. "Leave her alone, Judas. It was intended that she should save this perfume for the day of My burial. You will always have the poor among you, but you will not always have Me."

I love the way this family functioned so holistically together. If we work for integral mission, we will need integral lives. In this story – in this family - we see task, team and individual. We see service, relationship and intimacy. Martha served, Lazarus related, Mary worshipped. Martha worked, Lazarus networked, and Mary celebrated. Martha worked like she didn't need the money. Lazarus loved like he'd never been hurt. And Mary danced like no one was watching.

But that's my final point; people *were* watching. This family; this home church; this missional community; this Church Action Group; wasn't a clique, a members-only club, a gated neighbourhood, a party purely for the beautiful people or the socially acceptable. This family was prepared to live in the spotlight, welcoming into their home not only Jesus and a few close friends to celebrate with them, but also cynics and thieves and critics and crowds, and even persecutors.

I'd like to have a holistic life like that. I'd like to be a part of an integrated family like that. I'd like to be a part of a local church like that. I'd like to be a part of a local community like that, and I'd like (and this one takes a lot of faith) to be a part of a *nation* like that.

The Biblical Rationale

I've long been intrigued by Genesis 10. This is the chapter where suddenly and for the first time we read repeatedly of many different *structures* of society. Here (and I'm quoting from the NIV) we read of 'peoples, territories, clans, nations, languages, kingdoms, land, city, borders, region, country and nations'. With the exception of 'land' and one isolated reference to 'city', every one of these words gets its first biblical airing in Genesis chapter 10. Extraordinary! It is stuff that we all take for granted, but which is suddenly presented to us here, as the world and its population take shape.

However, 'family' is a concept that goes back even further. We read of Adam's family line in Genesis 5, and of Noah's family adventures in Genesis 6. In the next seven books of the Old Testament we can read specifically of the preserving of families, the building of families, the honour of families, the leaders and heads of families, the standards and banners of families, the registration, enrolment and counting of families, the responsibility of families, the traditions of families, the loyalty of families, and the inheritance of families. There are well over 300 specific references to family or families in the bible, and many, many more if you include words such as descendants, generations, children, fathers, mothers etc. There is no doubt that families are the core and most precious building block that God has given mankind to build our societies on.

"God sets the lonely in families" (Psalm 68:6 NIV). This is well illustrated in the book of Ruth, which is a beautiful story of covenant love as expressed through family. Widowed Ruth expressed a magnificent commitment to family when, despite it involving the crossing of cultures, she pleaded with her mother-in-law, *"Do not urge me to leave you or to turn back from you. Where you go I will go, and where you stay I will stay. Your people will be my people and your God my God. Where you die I will die, and there I will be buried. May the LORD deal with me, be it ever so severely, if even death separates you and me"* (Ruth 1:16-17 NIV). It was devotion like this which ultimately sustained a family line through which Jesus would be born something like thirty-one generations later.

In the Old Testament books of Samuel, Kings and Chronicles I have counted over 100 references (albeit with some repetition) to an individual being dealt honour or shame, blessing or curse, where the same was imposed upon his whole family. *"King David went in and sat before the Lord, and he said: 'Who am I, Sovereign Lord, and what is my family, that you have brought me this far?'"* (2 Samuel 7:18 NIV). Even the most important individual didn't see himself as an island, finding much of his identity in his family.

Nehemiah used families as the framework for his rebuilding and defence strategy (Nehemiah 4:13) and told the people not to fight for *him*, but to *"Remember the Lord, who is great and awesome, and fight for your families, your sons and your daughters, your wives and your homes."* (Nehemiah 4:14 NIV).

As we have seen already in this chapter, Jesus loved to be gathered up in family, especially in Martha, Lazarus and Mary's family. Also, and whenever He had the opportunity, He loved to talk about His Father and His Kingdom, and always with such honour, such respect. In fact, so determined was He to ensure that His followers belonged to and sought first the Family and the Kingdom of God, He was even ready to express the limits of earthly family commitment where it was in conflict with His Father's will and purpose (Luke 9:59-61).

In the epistles, the church is referred to as family (Galatians 6:10, I Thessalonians 4:10), and those who have given themselves to Christ as children of God (1 John 3:1). Sometimes even mentors and disciplers referred to themselves as fathers (1 Corinthians 4:15) and to their disciples as sons (2 Timothy 2:1).

Instruction is given as to how families should behave (I Timothy 3:4-5), with specific instruction and guidance given to wives (Ephesians 5:22-24, Colossian 3:18), to husbands (Ephesians 5:25-33, Colossian 3:19), to children (Ephesians 6:1-3, Colossians 3:20) and to fathers (Ephesians 6:4, Colossians 3:21).

The Raising Families Context

The families our churches work with come in many shapes and sizes. In reality, each family is unique. We work with child-headed households, and households headed by grandparents or by neighbours or by the church, all due to the disastrous results of HIV. We also have households consisting of grandparents and young children due to the parents' economic migration to lands far away. In some families the children care for their disabled parents, who are often the victims of stigma, discrimination and injustice. There are many families where one or even both parents have abandoned their children due to unfaithfulness, or the abuse of alcohol or drugs. We have families which have no settled home, but shelter where they can. Others live in straw houses, mud houses, others still in rented houses, very often with no locks on the door or security of tenure. In other cultures still we have families where several generations live together, sometimes under one roof and sometimes in compounds, or even in districts such as the Mahallas, social institutions built around family ties in certain parts of Central Asia and beyond. These are what the West would call 'extended households', a somewhat patronising expression that assumes our own model is the norm, and that larger households are therefore to be labelled differently. More honestly and humbly, I think we should perhaps describe ours as 'diminished households'.

Whatever its shape and size, biblically and socially, we see the family as a fundamental unit and building block for healthy societies. And so the *Raising Families* model envisions and challenges each church to commit to working with twenty of the most vulnerable families in their village or neighbourhood. Sometimes these families are referred or nominated to the church by local authorities and social services. However, although some such families are hidden away, very often the most vulnerable families have already been identified by and are already known to the church and the community at large.

Families that respond to the *Raising Families* programme and to the friendship and support of the local church can confidently anticipate that over three years they will learn the skills and receive the support necessary to see significant improvement to their lives in terms of their relationships, their health, their education, their livelihoods, their shelter and their protection. During this time many will come into a relationship with Jesus Christ through repentance and faith. But even if they don't, they will be left in no doubt that the church, motivated by the love of Christ, has served them well with open and good hearts. Random people in the neighbourhoods we work in are surveyed at the start and at the end of each three year programme cycle, and asked a simple question. "Which people or groups, if any, care for vulnerable families in your community?" It is a joy to see how many people in the marketplace can now see for themselves the way the church reaches out to the vulnerable.[13]

Training opportunities are numerous and tailored to each context, but typically the trainers (volunteer church members who have been trained themselves) will help resource families in their *relationships*; with God, with their community and their environment, with one another, and with themselves (i.e. their self-esteem).

In terms of improved *health*, families are helped to access health services, and taught common disease, hygiene and HIV awareness, first aid and nutrition. Regarding *education*, they are taught how to access education (and the mentor will often go to the school and advocate for the healthy inclusion of vulnerable and excluded children). Early child development, career guidance and adult learning are other educational ingredients of the training programme. In terms of *income generation* many will learn simple farming, sowing, cooking, production and marketing techniques, join a savings and loans scheme, and maybe be taught about fund-raising. And with regard to their *protection* and social wellbeing, families (very often for the first time) will learn about family planning, child protection, gender based violence, disability awareness, anti-trafficking and palliative care.

---

[13] Our survey results show that the "percentage of the population that acknowledge the church as active in reaching out to vulnerable families" increased from 56% to 96% in Rwanda (2013-16) and from 12% to 68% in Swaziland (2012-15)

It's not that every church will train on every aspect mentioned here, but these are some of the regularly trained topics that become the fabric of *shalom* that these families learn to wrap themselves in.

Testimonies from Raising Families Practitioners

The best parents in the world

Maxim is 37 years old. He and his wife Sveta (34) have two children, Anatoly (8) and Konstantin (3). One dark night in November 2015 Maxim and Sveta knocked at the door of the local pastor and *Raising Families* Action Group Leader's house. The pastor had known Sveta for few years. Most people did. She was usually at the market place, drunk. He had helped her with food and clothing for herself and children, and for years had witnessed to her about God. She did not want to hear him, but just took the food.

This night they came for help. It was bitterly cold outside, and they had nowhere to sleep. They asked to spend the night in the pastor's house. He let them in and fed them. The next day they bathed and were given clean clothes. Maxim and his family lived with the pastor's family for ten days. During this time Action

Group members witnessed to them again, and Maxim with Sveta opened their hearts to Jesus, making Him their Saviour.

The group members then found a farmer who needed somebody to look after their cattle. It would mean living in the cowshed, but Maxim and Sveta were very happy to get both a job and a place where they could live together with their children.

Their lives were changed. God set them free from alcohol addiction, and they started living better than before, in a clean and warm albeit very basic home, having proper nutrition for the children and for themselves. They now attend all the services and the trainings that take place in the church during the week and on Sundays.

Maxim told his wife that he would never have thought that the people of another nation (they are Russians and the pastor is Kyrgyz) could love and share their home with them. He said, "We are very grateful to the pastor and the Action Group for their love and care. We are glad that we can live together as a family and our children now have everything they need for good development." The children are happy that their parents do not drink or swear any more, and they say that they have the best parents in the world.

From hostility to service

Asel sat in her home and spoke of her wonderful story of reconciliation to God and her husband. After seriously regretting having been pressured into having an abortion, Asel started looking for God, praying and seeking Him. She visited witch doctors and Islamic leaders to no effect, but one day she cried to God, 'God if you really exist, and if you really are a living God, please come and help me'. On that very day she met a Christian lady who introduced her to the church. Asel started attending the church but couldn't fully understand what was going on. In her worldview, God should be rejecting and punishing her, but instead He seemed to be accepting and forgiving her!

"I became dreadfully sick and totally unable to walk, and doctors told me I was a hopeless case. I prayed and said, 'If you are the living God, the creator of the heaven and the earth, would you come and help me?' My temperature dropped and I started to walk again. It was a miracle. I came to my husband, Genish, and said, 'Look! I can walk, because I called on the name of Jesus!' I'd said, 'God if you heal me, nobody is going to stop me following you!'"

"Having accepted Jesus Christ as my Saviour, my husband became hostile towards me and God, and banned me from going to church. He would lock me inside the house so that I couldn't go. He invited thirty relatives to come and persuade me to deny Christ. Burial ceremonies are so important to our Kyrgyz roots, and so they beat me and threatened that no one would bury me if

I didn't deny Christ. Finally, at 1am, they just threw me out of the house. I took our recently-adopted baby with me, but Genish found me, took the baby away, and would still come and beat me up regularly."

"My husband married again, but I prayed for three years for the restoration of my family. I prayed and fasted for forty days, and God answered this prayer and brought Genish back to me. One day God told me, 'It's not really about you. I am choosing Genish for My glory, and I'm going to meet him very soon.' So when Genish divorced his wife, and re-married me a year ago, he accepted Jesus Christ, which was a big shock for our relatives."

Genish sat peaceably while his wife spoke openly of his previous violence, rejection and unfaithfulness. He wondered gratefully at the grace of God now on him, which had made him so accepting of this testimony, parts of which focused onto his own shortcomings. He realised that his repentance and faith had gone deep, and he was no longer ashamed. At last Genish joined in the conversation. "We don't really have any connection with the relatives right now because they still cannot accept what has happened to us. They were so surprised when I came to Jesus. They were in shock, and still are. They mocked me and said, 'the one who was most against Jesus became the first to accept Him.'"

"When I threw my wife out, I found another wife, but I would come home and find both her and my dad totally drunk. They started selling items from the house, arguing and drinking more, so finally I started drinking as well. Twice I was in serious car accidents because I was drunk. I then realised and accepted that God needed me, because He rescued me both times without injury, although my car was totally wrecked and my passengers were badly injured."

"Finally we divorced and I came back to find Asel. I visited her several times, asking her what I should do for her to come back to me. When I visited her on her birthday, several church members were there. Through all this time I was praying to God, and asking Him where He was and that I needed help. I told Him, 'I can't do life on my own.' He heard my prayer and I came back to Asel, and I asked her to call her new friends because I was ready to receive Jesus Christ. They came and I received Jesus. So then we had to go through the marriage process again, and here we are, praise God, officially man and wife again!"

"When I came to Jesus, God clearly spoke to me from the scriptures. He said, 'You did not choose Me but I chose you!' He told me that I'd been chosen since my mother's womb! I was a very sick child, and doctors said I wouldn't live long and that I would be mentally sick. I wouldn't live or prosper. So God really spoke to me through these verses, about how much I need God, and about how much He needs me! This is why He saved my life and healed me. He has purpose for my life!"

Asel went on to describe how much she wants to serve the Lord, and how excited she was when her church began to serve the homeless people of their community through the *Raising Families* programme.

"It was four years ago when I started praying for the homeless people. Living on our own, me and my little boy were really struggling and didn't have food enough for us. But one day my son, then five years old, said to me, "Let's share our food with the homeless people," so we did. We started feeding homeless people, and still do so today. I started cooking from what I had, and began feeding them, especially the women, bringing food to the basement where they were living."

"My main idea was not just to feed these people but to listen to them, to ask them why and how homelessness happened in their lives. Every time I visit them it is amazing, as God gives me a new person each time to talk with. We've become really good friends. They greet me and say, 'Oh Asel, darling!' when I arrive."

These days Genish and Asel continue to grow spiritually, and faithfully serve in the *Raising Families* programme, Asel continuing to work with the homeless, and Genish serving as a driver and as a trainer for new workers. Recently they conducted a fundraising campaign in a nearby town to urge wealthy tourists and businessmen to support poor families by providing school supplies for their children.

"Therefore if anyone is in Christ, the new creation has come: the old has gone, the new is here! All this is from God, who reconciled us to himself through Christ and gave us the ministry of reconciliation." 2 Corinthians 5:17-18 NIV

Questions for Group Discussion

- Are families in other cultures 'extended', or is the typical Western family unit 'diminished'? What's normal? Discuss.

- How regularly are families the focus of the main 'Sunday teaching' in our church, and how well does our church train families through other programmes, resources and support?

- What other Christian agencies, networks and forums are there in our town which could help support the growth of healthy family life, and what could our church do to partner with them more?

- If our church gave each family the opportunity to stand together in front of the congregation and testify to what

God had done for you together in the last four weeks, what would your family agree to share?

- UK children are now more likely to have a smartphone than a father at home. And, if current trends remain as they are, any child born today in the UK has only a 50/50 chance of being with both their birth parents by the age of 15.[14] Our media regularly reports on the desperate shortage of houses, and yet more people than ever live on their own. Why is this so, what does it say about our culture, and what could be done about it?

- Martha served, Lazarus related, Mary worshipped. Martha worked, Lazarus networked, and Mary celebrated. Martha worked like she didn't need the money. Lazarus loved like he'd never been hurt. And Mary danced like no one was watching. How would you describe the way the members of your household complement one another?

- There is no evidence that 'the family that Jesus loved' included anyone who was married or had children. If you are single, or are living on your own, how have you felt whilst reading this chapter and working through these questions, and how could others in the group understand, include and support you more?

---

[14] http://marriagefoundation.org.uk/research/

Study Eight

The Focus on the Poor

Why we should aim to walk with the most marginalised

What exactly *is* poverty?

Ask a room full of people to define poverty, and some will quote statistics, others will go practical, and others still will offer a more emotional response. 'Absolute poverty' (i.e. a set standard which is consistent over time and between countries) was a concept introduced in 1990 and defined as people living on $1 per day. This figure was reset by the World Bank at $1.90 per day in 2015, which estimated that year 702 million people, or 9.6% of the world's population, were living in absolute poverty.[15] The UN claimed the figure was more like 836 million.[16]

Relative poverty, however, whilst meaning a lot to those to whom it relates, is an entirely different thing. A UK household is in 'relative poverty' if its income is below 60% of the median household income, which according to the Department of Work

---

[15] http://www.worldbank.org/en/news/press-release/2015/10/04/world-bank-forecasts-global-poverty-to-fall-below-10-for-first-time-major-hurdles-remain-in-goal-to-end-poverty-by-2030
[16] http://www.un.org/sustainabledevelopment/poverty/

and Pensions was £481 per week (before housing costs) in 2015-16.[17]

When describing the depths of poverty around the world, the descriptions 'absolute', 'extreme', 'ultra-' and 'abject' are more or less synonymous. The UN declaration at the World Summit on Social Development in Copenhagen in 1995 stated that extreme poverty is "a condition characterized by severe deprivation of basic human needs, including food, safe drinking water, sanitation facilities, health, shelter, education and information. It depends not only on income but also on access to services."[18]

I'm glad for the inclusion of the words 'information' and 'access' in this description. An understanding of the huge need for these 'invisibles' is crucial for those seeking to do something about it. For me the word that most weightily describes poverty is 'powerlessness'. Whatever the problem, it is people's inability to do anything about it that can lock them permanently and hopelessly into that state.

So poverty takes on many forms. There are the obvious, tangible ones, which we could call 'physical poverty', and which include lack of wealth (i.e. material wealth such as food, clothing,

---

[17] http://researchbriefings.files.parliament.uk/documents/CBP-7484/CBP-7484.pdf
[18] http://www.un.org/esa/socdev/wssd/text-version/agreements/poach2.htm

housing, resources) and lack of health (i.e. physical health such as sickness, disease, disability, frailty etc).

Then there is 'spiritual poverty'. Being poor in our relationship with or towards God, or being spiritually dull, hard of hearing God and unable to respond to Him. Interestingly, this possibly impacts the physically rich even more than the physically poor, a subject well worth exploring elsewhere.

But what other forms of poverty are there? Well there is 'emotional poverty'. Being poor in relationship with or towards myself, having low self-esteem, lacking 'shalom', or being unable to maintain a position of faith, peace and inner contentment.

Then there is 'social (or relational) poverty'. Being poor in relationships with or towards those with whom I have a meaningful relationship. Being unable to relate comfortably and consistently with people around me (my family, church members, work colleagues, neighbours etc) without conflict, resulting in loneliness, divorce, abuse, alienation, dismissal, disconnection etc.

And then there is 'political (or societal) poverty'. Being poor in my relationship with or towards society. The state of powerlessness, lacking access, opportunity (e.g. to documents, registration, health, education, employment etc), freedom and or power to change my circumstances. Under this heading we could include living under persecution or injustice, or being displaced, either internally (IDPs), or internationally (refugees).

When it comes to the lifting of ourselves out of poverty, in general terms I would suggest that our society would probably prioritise this firstly in terms of *material* wealth, and then *physical* health, and thirdly maybe a societal concern over *human rights*. *Emotional* wholeness and improved *relationships* might typically make up the top five aspects of poverty considered to be worth addressing.

The typical church pastor, however, might view things a little differently. It's another sweeping statement of course, but at a guess most of his or her sermons would probably focus primarily on overcoming *spiritual* poverty, then *physical* health or healing, maybe followed from time to time by something that addressed the breakdown of *relationships*, and occasionally would offer comment or advice on issues of *wealth* and *human rights*.

In the 'Biblical Rationale' below, we'll see how Jesus approached the issue of poverty. But in completing this introduction, let me make reference to a quote from Jesus that has long intrigued me. Was He being faithless, or resigned, when He said, *"the poor you will always have with you"*? (Matthew 26:11, Mark 14:7 NIV). Was it just an incidental, throw away comment to introduce what He really wanted to say, about His anointing for burial? I think there is more to it than that.

Our society is ruthless, driven, task-focussed, cynical, irritable and impatient, and puts me under increasing pressure to perform, to perform *well*, and to perform *now*. Where I cannot manage to do this, I am deemed to be 'non-productive' and a burden. And yet, I suggest to you, our society desperately *needs* those who are vulnerable, those who not only need discipleship but genuinely need care and support. The frail elderly, the orphan, the widow, the refugee, and those with mental ill health. The church is a 'hospital', a 'school' and an 'army' in equal measure. Let it train brilliantly and let it fight hard, but let it offer healing as well. "*I desire mercy*," says the Lord (Hosea 6:6 NIV).

I *need* those who are perceived to be vulnerable, as much as they need me. If I don't have those who are vulnerable within my close sphere of friends and neighbours, all too easily I become selfish, cliquey, and thin of spirit. I settle for being purely functional, an exclusive gated community and an Aryan race, a competitive machine that abandons relationship for the sake of striving for 'results', 'success' and 'continual improvement'. God help us! No wonder stress-related sick leave is on the increase.

If you count yourself among the 'poor' as you read this (i.e. poor in pocket, poor in spirit, poor in mind, poor in body), I salute you, I honour you, and I give you great respect. By allowing yourself to be vulnerable and to receiving support, you not only exhibit great grace (for most of us find it really *hard* to receive), but you also serve me and rescue me from my self-centred functionality. You offer our society the opportunity to show *mercy*, and to give ourselves away for one another, and thus vastly improve it.

The Biblical Rationale

In his book *Together Again,* Roger S. Greenway[19] reflects that "Throughout the scriptures we can read of a bias towards the poor. The Old Testament makes it abundantly clear that care for the poor and the protection of the innocent against injustice were essential elements in covenant life. The destitute and disabled, widows, orphans and sojourners (refugees) are singled out by Old Testament writers as worthy of and in need of special consideration by God's people. In Exodus 21-33 we find the oldest prescriptions on covenant responsibility. God said to His people

- Do not mistreat an alien or oppress him, for you were aliens in Egypt (Exodus 22:21)
- Do not take advantage of a widow or orphan. If you do and they cry out to me, I will certainly hear their cry (Exodus 22:22-23)
- Do not deny justice to your poor people in their lawsuits (Exodus 23:6)"

---

[19] Together again: kinship of word and deed; Roger S. Greenway, 1998

The prophet Amos spoke against those who "trample the poor" (2:7, 5:11), "crush the needy" (4:1) and "buy or sell the poor with silver" or for a pair of sandals (2:6, 8:6). *"Defend the cause of the fatherless, plead the case of the widow"*, urged Isaiah (1:17 NIV), and he lamented over the bribe-loving and rebellious rulers who did not do these things (1:23). King Josiah was praised by Jeremiah (22:16 NIV) because he *"defended the cause of the poor and needy",* citing this as the reason that all went well with him. *"'Is that not what it means to know me?' declares the Lord."*

Jesus, the early church and many mission and renewal movements throughout New Covenant history have opened their hearts and arms wide to seek to compassionately address the needs of the poor. In the New Testament, Tabitha (Acts 9:36), Cornelius (Acts 10:4), and the Christians in Macedonia and Achaia (Romans 15:26-27) were all praised for their determination to meet the needs of the poor. Jesus' brother James (in James 2) had very tough things to say to any church that discriminated against (v4) or dishonoured (v6) or showed favouritism against (v9) or was without mercy towards (v13) the poor.

As already discussed, Jesus' statement that *"the poor you will always have with you"* (Mark 14:7 NIV) was not defeatist. Rather it was a reminder of His eternal heart for the most vulnerable in society. And it was a reminder that our attitude towards the poor will ultimately be a matter of life and death.

To the righteous, to walk with the poor is second nature. With some naïve puzzlement and with innocence of spirit they will one day say, *""Lord, when did we see you hungry and feed you, or thirsty and give you something to drink? When did we see you a stranger and invite you in, or needing clothes and clothe you? When did we see you ill or in prison and visit you?" And the King will reply, "Truly, I tell you, whatever you did for one of the most vulnerable (least) of these brothers and sisters of mine, you did it to me.""* (Matthew 25:39-40 NIV).

Once Jesus went to Nazareth, where He had been brought up. It was the Sabbath day and, as was His custom, He went into the synagogue. There He stood up to read, and the scroll of the prophet Isaiah was handed to Him. Unrolling it, He found the place in Isaiah (61:1-3) where it is written:

"The Spirit of the Lord is on me, because he has anointed me to proclaim good news to the poor. He has sent me to proclaim freedom for the prisoners and recovery of sight for the blind, to set the oppressed free, to proclaim the year of the Lord's favour."

Then He rolled up the scroll, gave it back to the attendant and sat down, ready to teach. The wide eyes of everyone in the synagogue were fastened on Him, and a shiver of anticipation and expectation went down their spines as He looked up and told them, *"Today, this scripture is fulfilled in your hearing."*

155

Basically Jesus had said, "Look I'm interested in saving you from absolutely every aspect of the poverty that holds you down, be it spiritual, physical, material, emotional, relational or societal." In these two simple sentences (Luke 4:18-19 NIV) Jesus addresses the needs of the poor, of prisoners, the blind and the oppressed. He does so by means of the Spirit of the Lord, proclaiming (mentioned three times), recovering, and releasing, resulting in good news, freedom, recovery, sight and release.

No-one had expected anything special that day. It was the same old home town (Nazareth), just another Sunday (Sabbath), the same old church service (synagogue), and the same old bible reading (Isaiah 61). But through this one scripture Jesus outlined a radically new approach to life, the purposes and the Kingdom of God on earth. He demonstrated God's holistic interest in the well-being of *every* part of people's lives, and He would go on through the cross to rescue people from *every* form of poverty. No wonder the eyes of all were fastened on Him.

The Raising Families Context

From the start of the *Raising Families* envisioning programme, we emphasise and seek to build an understanding of poverty on "The Four Relationships", which borrows significantly from the work of Bryant L. Myers and his book, "Walking with the Poor".[20]

The four relationships can be summarised as

1. Our relationship with God
2. Our relationship with self
3. Our relationship with others and the community
4. Our relationship with the environment and creation

When they are broken, the poverty that ensues is

1. Spiritual
2. Emotional and mental
3. Social and political
4. Material and economic

We look at the root causes of poverty, going back to the beginning of time, and we seek to build an understanding in the churches and families we work with as to who God is and what He intended for the world. It soon becomes very clear that poverty is *not* what He wanted. We look together at the concept of *'shalom'*, or the wholeness and completeness that comes when all these relationships are in harmony with one another.

When the Church Action Groups have been envisioned, trained and equipped to serve their communities, they complete a community needs- and an asset-assessment, and commit to working alongside twenty of the most vulnerable families in their neighbourhoods. If I were to summarise the five practical building

---

[20] Walking With The Poor: Principles and Practices of Transformational Development; Bryant L. Myers

blocks of support which these poor families can anticipate help with, as they lift themselves out of poverty, I would categorise them as follows:

1. Health (spiritual, physical, food security, nutrition, access to health services)
2. Education (school, training)
3. Livelihoods (employment, income generation, diversity of income)
4. Shelter (safe, affordable, adequate shelter)
5. Protection (from violence, abuse and neglect)

You will recall that the expression I used in my introduction to this chapter was 'absolute' or 'extreme poverty'. It should be noted that many of the churches we work with have a majority of their own members living in 'extreme poverty'. Indeed, many such people are fully functioning members of our Church Action Groups, reaching out with love and sacrifice to other vulnerable families in their communities. How can this be? Surely such people are consumed with their own troubles, and have no resources to reach out to others? Well, 'extreme poverty' is actually a biblical expression, used by Paul, and it is one which reminds me so much of these brothers and sisters of mine in Uganda, Rwanda, Zambia, Swaziland and Kyrgyzstan. When talking of the Macedonian churches in 2 Corinthians 8:2-5 (NIV), Paul says, "*In the midst of a very severe trial, their overflowing joy and their extreme poverty welled up in rich generosity. For I testify that they gave as much as they were able, and even beyond their ability....: they gave themselves first of all to the Lord, and then by the will of God also to us."*

We recently completed a sustainability review that, among other things, tested the premise that "The (*RaFa*) programme is targeted at the poorest (most vulnerable), and impartially (gender, children, ethnicity, disability, faith etc)". With an exceptional score of 95%, the narrative conclusion stated that *"All RaFa programmes scored exceptionally high on this sub-heading. The poorest make up almost all the participants, and experience the most significant change of all involved. Participants are from a broad spectrum of marginalised groups, including child-headed households, single-parent households, the homeless, the destitute, the frail elderly, those with mental ill health, physical and learning disability etc. Despite being overtly Christian, the programme makes no distinction of religion with regard to the selection of families to work with, and families broadly reflect the religious and ethnic community mix."*[21]

Actually, many of the churches interviewed expressed puzzlement as to why the question was even being asked, due to the intrinsic nature of the gospel and of this programme to walk with the poorest in society. "Of course we do!" they exclaimed. "It's what we are here for".

---

[21] CIDOS review; Samaritan's Purse UK, 2017

Testimonies from Raising Families Practitioners

From the hundreds of testimonies that we could have chosen for this chapter, here are a selection of stories from Uganda.

I'm alive today because of the compassion and love of Christ

Abonyo Jerolina is 80 years old. She has no children, and she lost her husband 10 years ago. Her condition was bad. She could not walk and was too weak to go to the hospital for treatment. The hut she called home was in a sorry state, and no neighbour offered to help her. Her surviving siblings live far from her home and her life had become dependent on occasional well-wishers who passed her compound. Many times Jerolina cried alone in the house. With no help, she had lost hope in life completely.

After being trained in the *Raising Families* programme, one local church called Ogwangadar Church of Uganda in Aboke Parish, Kole District, identified Jerolina as one who desperately needed support and compassionate care.

The Church members came and began by repairing her grass thatched house, which was at the state of falling over her and threatening her life. Sometimes they provided a motorcycle to carry her to church for prayers on Sundays, and to the nearby health centre for treatment. Two members of the group volunteered to routinely help with the house work. A few selected church members started organising fellowship in her home to pray and have bible study. Her neighbours were touched through this Christian fellowship and, having seen the love being demonstrated by church members, they too started cooking food, cleaning the compound, and washing the utensils for Jerolina.

Jerolina is grateful to the Church for their concern and generosity in caring for and supporting vulnerable people that are suffering in the community, without discrimination. *"I'm alive today because of the compassion and love of Christ extended to me through the church. My faith has been strengthened and hope restored in the Lord Jesus,"* she says.

Restored back into the community

Evas Bakainama is 56 years old, a widow living in Kihagani Village in Masindi District, Uganda. Nine of her eleven children are still alive. She lived with two of her youngest sons and four of her grandchildren, but she had no means of livelihood and struggled to meet the basic needs of her family members. Their home was a dilapidated shelter, not fit for human living, and the children had dropped out of school. At this point Evas became worried and started falling sick with tuberculosis and malaria and became very weak, living at the mercy of well-wishers for handouts.

Whilst the Kihagani CAG were completing a community assessment, the leader of the group reached Evas' home and found her bedridden. At this point Evas had tested HIV positive and was losing hope in life. The CAG visited Evas and encouraged her to visit the health centre for treatment. She agreed and was enrolled on the life prolonging anti-retroviral treatment.

Since then the CAG members have been very supportive to Evas. They provided spiritual counselling, transport to the hospital, food and other items to support this family for a while. Through this kind of support Evas became healthy and strong. And so then the church encouraged her to engage in some simple livelihood activity to help her generate food and income for the family.

She started digging to raise food for the family. Later she started a poultry project. Evas is able now to sell the birds to meet the needs of the family and pay for her medical treatment.

"I thank God and the Church and Diocese for introducing this programme that looks after vulnerable people, and especially for restoring me back in the community. I have accepted Jesus Christ as my Lord and personal saviour, and I am now an active member of the Church. I was even elected the Treasurer!" she says.

Restoring the poles that the termites had eaten

Amos and Nora are an elderly Christian couple living in Oyam District, Northern Uganda. They lived in a constant state of worry about the state of their home, which was almost collapsing. Their house had a grass rooftop, which attracted termites which ate into support poles. These poles were bending so much it appeared as if they would fall at any moment. Major repairs were nearly impossible for Amos and Nora. They bore no children of their own to offer labour to support them, and their land is far from other relatives.

In Amos and Nora's community *Raising Families* trained church members that formed Church Action Groups (CAGs), which then penetrated their local communities to offer practical care to the vulnerable. One such group trained in this community is called *'Agenrwot', or 'Trust God'*. Whilst doing their community care outreach, this group identified Amos and Nora as one of the vulnerable families to be cared for and supported.

The CAG members noted the issues with Nora and Amos' house, but also saw they had been sick and needed urgent medical attention. They prayed together and collected money amongst themselves to support the couple to go for medical treatment, following which their health improved greatly. The CAG members then turned their attention to the housing problem. Locally they found the required materials that could be obtained to do the house construction. Women in the CAG brought grass and water.

Men moulded blocks and cut poles for hut construction. Working together, the CAG completed this work within a week.

"I thought when the rains come that we shall not make it, because I am weak and cannot manage alone to construct a house for my wife, but God is good to us. He has given us a new house through these people", said Amos joyfully.

God has shown Amos and Nora that even without children of their own, they are provided for, and that He is their Provider. The couple is already gratefully living in the house. Through this type of ministry outreach, the CAGs are supporting many families with desperate needs in their communities.

Questions for Group Discussion

- Quietly write down words or very short expressions that you personally think best describe 'poverty'.
- Now share them with each other, one at a time around the room, and discuss.
- Briefly describe to the group where it was that you saw poverty that shocked you the most.
- Do people in the UK *need* to be poor?
- Apart from the informal initiatives of individuals, does your church have programmes or other organised forms

of commitment that specifically address the needs of the poor in your community?

- Come to a point of agreement in your group as to what percentage of your church's income you think should be invested into the poor.

- Do you know what percentage of your church's income *is* invested into the poor?

- When people in the street ask you, "Have you got any spare change?" what do you feel, how do you respond, and why do you respond this way?

- Paul said, *"If I give all I possess to the poor…. but do not have love, I gain nothing"* (1 Corinthians 13:3). Discuss the different motives of (e.g.) pity, duty, obligation and love, and carefully consider together what love will achieve that the others don't.

- "Being spiritually dull, hard of hearing and being unable to respond to Him personally impacts the physically rich even more than the physically poor". Do you agree? Why do you answer this way?

Study Nine

Enduring Hardship

Pressing on in the face of trouble

If only....

If only I could win the lottery. If only I was a little younger. If only I was a little older. If only I had a job. If only I had more time. If only I was married. If only I was single. There always seems to be *one* thing which we think we need, and which we haven't got, which all too easily becomes the *only* thing that stops us doing the *very* thing that God wants us to do!

It is my enormous privilege to work alongside people who have determined not to make the thing they lack an excuse for not doing the will of God. Consequently I count among my best friends those who have been victims of genocide, war and other atrocities. Some have survived rape and torture, or have lost their homes and family, or have become either internally displaced or refugees. They tell their stories with much pain, but also with such faith and mercy, and with a calm resolve to seek a better future.

> *"When I said, 'My foot is slipping,' your unfailing love, Lord, supported me. When anxiety was great within me, your consolation brought me joy."* Psalm 94:18-19 NIV

Others among my most precious acquaintances live realistically and repeatedly in anticipation of being ostracised, antagonised and persecuted. In some places this takes the form of a consistent, strategic and systematic form of opposition from central government institutions, and in other locations it can come more randomly and unpredictably from resentful and volatile neighbours and relations. One is like a constant driving rain from which you cannot escape, and the other is like a sudden flash flood or a thunderstorm that appears violently and without warning. One is more wearying and the other is more frightening. But the love of Christ controls these friends of mine, and even though some have watched while their peers have fled, even emigrating to seek calmer futures elsewhere, others accept that these are the conditions in which God continues to call them to live and work.

"If you have no opposition in the place you serve, you are serving in the wrong place," said G Campbell Morgan, a long time ago.

Not everyone involved in *Raising Families* experiences war or persecution. Some merely contend with desperate poverty, in all its forms. We took a detailed look in the previous chapter at the whole issue of poverty, but enough for me to say here that these friends of mine who have lived their lives in ultra-poverty are some of the most generous, grateful and contented people I know. When drought badly hit Swaziland in 2016, I went back to my colleagues and suggested that we temporarily change the approach of *Raising Families* from one of asset-based development to more of an aid or hand-out model. They begged me not to. "If ever there was a time for the church to love its neighbours and to serve them sacrificially, then this is it", I was unequivocally told.

Be it epidemics such as HIV and AIDS as well as drought (as in Swaziland), or the threat of Islamic extremism, drugs and human trafficking (as in Central Asia), or mass unemployment following the collapse of the mining industry (as in Zambia), or the 1994 genocide and ethnic cleansing (as in Rwanda), or the destructive impact of the LRA (as in Northern Uganda), every nation we work in is either trying to recover from something terrible in their recent past, or fighting to ensure that pending disasters don't hit them too hard in the future. This is the setting in which our *Raising Families* programme operates, facilitated by Christ-like women and men who determine not to put limitations upon God or themselves, but to 'face the music and dance'.

If only... If only we could be like that in the Church in the UK.

The Biblical Rationale

I guess it is references of 'suffering' that we are most likely to think of when looking at this subject. Suffering is like the biblical word for aggro. Virtually every writer and book in the New Testament (interestingly, with the exception of John, both in his gospel or his epistles) has something to say about it. And yet in this chapter, by way of a change, I will focus instead on the words 'trouble' and 'hardship'.

There are about 172 references to 'trouble' in the bible, and a quarter of them are in the book of Psalms. Unsurprisingly, another 17 of these are in the book of Job. Wherever we look, the scriptures leave us in no doubt that trouble ain't far away.

Jesus personally knew deep distress and trouble (Mark 14:33, John 11:33). He told us we would to. *"In this world you will have trouble"* He said (John 16:33 NIV), and, *"Each day has enough trouble of its own"* (Matthew 6:34 NIV). He told His disciples that 25% of the seeds they sow will actually take no lasting root due to trouble or persecution (Matthew 13:21).

I don't recall Jesus ever telling us to keep *out* of trouble. Biblically, 'keeping out of trouble' was the sole preserve of those guards who wanted to cover their tracks when Jesus' body was found to be no longer in the tomb (Matthew 28:14).

Rather than avoiding trouble, Jesus told us what to do when trouble comes our way.

- *"Do not worry"* (Matthew 6:34 NIV)
- *"Stay here and keep watch with me"* (Matthew 26:38 NIV)
- *"Watch and pray so that you will not fall into temptation"* (Mark 14:38 NIV)
- *"Look at my hands and my feet. It is I myself! Touch me and see"* (Luke 24:38-39 NIV)
- *"Trust in God; trust also in me"* (John 14:1 NIV)
- *"I go and prepare a place for you, I will come back and take you to be with me, that you also may be where I am"* (John 14:3 NIV)
- *"The Holy Spirit… will teach you all things and will remind you of everything I have said to you"* (John 14:26 NIV)
- *"My peace I give you… do not be afraid"* (John 14:27 NIV)
- *"Take heart"* (John 16:33 NIV)

All these instructions are given as a *direct* response to trouble that His followers were in. In summary there were three fundamental directives He repeatedly gave them. Trust in me. I'll give you the words to say. I will never leave you. More or less the same as God said to Moses at the burning bush (Exodus 3-4), when He called Moses to respond to *"the misery of my people in Egypt"* (3:7 NIV). Do not be afraid (3:6, 10, 14). I will be with you (3:12). I will teach you what to say (4:12).

And when the deepest trouble of all (i.e. His imminent death on the cross for the sins of the whole world) was staring Him in the face, Jesus weighed His options (John 12:27-28 NIV). Back out or press on? He said to His Father, *"Now my soul is troubled, and what shall I say? 'Father, save me from this hour'? No, it was for this very reason I came to this hour. Father, glorify your name!"* Our pioneer, our hero, our ultimate example! Hallelujah! We should not be surprised that His Father, overwhelmed with pride and love for His son, could not remain silent (John 12:28 NIV). *"Then a voice came from heaven, 'I have glorified it, and will glorify it again.'"*

In his support to the churches in Lystra, Iconium and Antioch, Paul was *"strengthening the disciples and encouraging them to remain true to the faith. 'We must go through many hardships to enter the Kingdom of God'"* he said (Acts 14:22 NIV).

In fact Paul was convinced that it was not possible for him to be separated from the love of Christ, be it by trouble or hardship or persecution or famine or nakedness or danger or sword. Even if he were to face death all day long, or be considered as sheep to be slaughtered, his living testimony was that *"in all these things we are more than conquerors through him who loved us. For I am*

171

convinced that neither death nor life, neither angels nor demons, neither the present nor the future, nor any powers, neither height nor depth, nor anything else in all creation, will be able to separate us from the love of God that is in Christ Jesus our Lord" (Romans 8:35-39 NIV).

Later, and *"compelled by the Spirit"*, Paul set off for Jerusalem, *"not knowing what will happen to me there. I only know that in every city the Holy Spirit warns me that prison and hardships are facing me. However, I consider my life worth nothing to me; my only aim is to finish the race and complete the task the Lord Jesus has given me..."* (Acts 20:22-24 NIV).

He laid the same message on thick in his second letter to the Corinthians. Whether the believers in Corinth were settling for the easy life or not I don't know, but his letter, which is like a very unusual c.v., talks liberally of his sufferings (1:5) experiences (4:8), appeals (5:20), commendations (6:4), reports (6:8), testimonies (8:3), and even offers some foolishness (11:1) and boasting (11:16-33), all based on the dreadful treatment he had received for being a disciple of Christ. But he was far from moaning. And he wasn't simply *tolerating* his circumstances either. Nearing the end of his letter (12:10 NIV) he concludes, *"I delight in weaknesses, in insults, in hardships, in persecutions, in difficulties. For when I am weak, then I am strong."*

We know our bibles. Many of us have read these things before. But maybe they are worth some quiet reflection. Was it for our own peace and comfort that we accepted Christ, or did we urge Him to accept us as His disciples, come what may? It's a challenging question. My *Raising Families* friends in other lands are certainly doing that, and are still reaching out to others despite their own struggles. If the UK church can grasp something of their spirit and determination, we will have learned well. Timothy was urged to endure hardship (2 Timothy 4:5), as were the Hebrews (Hebrews 12:7), and the church in Ephesus was praised by Jesus (described here as *'someone like a son of man'* Revelation 1:13 NIV) for having *"endured hardships for my name"* (Revelation 2:3 NIV).

Raising Families Context

What are the particular hardships that are being faced by my *Raising Families* colleagues, and the nations and regions they are from?

Swaziland

The aforementioned drought in Swaziland is not the only major issue the nation has been facing. And nor is the fact that 69% of the population live below the poverty line.[22] HIV and AIDS,

---

[22] CIA World Factbook

coupled with a high rate of co-infection with tuberculosis, caused life expectancy in The Kingdom of Swaziland to be halved in the first decade of the millennium. Life expectancy was 61 in 2000 but then dropped to 32 in 2009.[23] With the highest prevalence of HIV as a percentage of 19-49 year olds in the world,[24] HIV and AIDS remains one of the major challenges to Swaziland's socioeconomic development. As an add-on component of our health training it is essential, therefore, that the *Raising Families* programme in Swaziland gives focussed instruction on HIV awareness. To monitor and reflect on the effectiveness of the trainings, our trainers return to these rural communities to ask eleven basic questions covering awareness, attitudes and good practice. Present results indicate that on average we are being 89.6% successful. Impressive maybe, but there's still some way to go to change some fringe behaviours, attitudes and practices.

Rwanda

Much has been written about the 1994 genocide in Rwanda. 300 people died every hour, night and day, for one hundred days. Probably 800,000 people in all lost their lives. Thousands of young adults now live and have to find their identity in the knowledge that they are the outcome of rape. And as with Swaziland and due to a spike in HIV infection, many households are still headed by orphaned children, widows and the elderly.

---

[23] UN Human Development Index
[24] 26.5% in 2012: World Bank

Needless to say the impact of genocide on the nation has been enormously profound and, albeit much of it unspoken, deep scars and pain will remain for a lifetime and well beyond.

And yet Rwanda is now in a very different place. This beautiful country of 'One Thousand Hills' now has a strong sense of order and backbone. Health, safety and environmental laws, such as the banning of plastic bags, the compulsory wearing of crash helmets when motor-cycling, and the adherence to strict speed limits, are all actually implemented and, in the main, obeyed. Inevitably, not everyone is in favour of this strong 'top-down' approach to leadership and governance, but it would appear to have been a means of bringing the country to where it is today. I pray that peace will prevail and that wholesome development will continue to revitalise the nation.

The Anglican Church, which is our long-term lead partner in Rwanda, has its own hierarchical structure as well, and one which has been a wonderful framework for effectiveness. His Grace the Archbishop of Rwanda has been fully involved and incredibly supportive of the programme, which at a national level has been a means of unity for the gathering of different confessions, and at a local level means that pastors and church activists have an almost inherent respect for *Raising Families* from the outset.

Our Church Action Groups continue to work in desperately poor rural communities, and it is a joy to see their members enduring hardships and constantly testifying about the goodness of God in their land.

Zambia

With a worldwide Human Development Index ranking of 139, Zambia is the location of our newest *Raising Families* programme, which is dedicated to working in the Copperbelt region of the country.

Our partners are based in Ndola, the country's third largest city. With a population of approaching half a million, and just 10km from the border with DR Congo, Ndola is the industrial and commercial centre of the Copperbelt region, and the capital of Copperbelt Province. The once highly profitable Bwana Mkubwa open-cast mine is only 10km from the city. With copper exports providing 70-80% of Zambia's export earnings, Ndola would surely seem a strange place to position a *Raising Families* programme.

But these days the townships of Ndola are looking anything but profitable. Bwana Mkubwa, the oldest mine in the country, and where there is evidence of mining operations going back to the fourteenth and fifteenth centuries, functions no longer. Operations were suspended in October 2008, with the plant placed on 'care and maintenance'. Attempts to revive it failed and it was formally closed in August 2010. It's a story repeated in many communities around the world, but in this community, our *RaFa* partners, who have great experience in vocational and entrepreneurial training of young people, are working with pastors and vulnerable families to seek new ways to generate income and establish themselves once more with dignity and purpose.

Uganda

Twenty-six minutes. That's the time it took Uganda to take in as many refugees as Japan took in during the whole of 2016. According to the UN Refugee Agency, Uganda took in 489,000 South Sudanese refugees in 2016, to say nothing of the steady flow from DR Congo and Burundi. In the same year, Japan took in 28 refugees.[25] Uganda took in more refugees in 2016 than any other country in the world. Many of them are settling in the North West of Uganda, receiving land and seeking to start a new life from scratch.

This is where the *RaFa* programme in Uganda has its focus, on the North Western Anglican Diocese of Masindi-Kitara and West Lango. It is a region that has known its own turmoil and trauma over the last few decades. Many will remember the impact of the Lord's Resistance Army, a violent 'Christian' cult, whose leader is Joseph Kony. The LRA has widely been accused of widespread human rights violations, including murder, mutilation, abduction, child sex-slavery and the forcing of children to participate in hostilities. I only too clearly recall hearing the first hand

[25] https://www.reuters.com/article/us-japan-asylum/japan-took-in-just-28-refugees-in-2016-despite-record-applications-idUSKBN15O0UV

testimonies of traumatised villagers who were told they must not collect the bodies of their murdered children from the local school, or they too would be butchered to death. Up to 15,000 rural children walked into the city of Gulu each night for months, in an attempt to sleep free of the fear of abduction. For a while the global media headlined with the shocking stories of these 'invisible children' or 'night commuters'.

And so after a truce had been signed in August 2006, hundreds of NGOs moved in to support the restoration and stability of the region. But with so many agencies providing hand-outs, sitting fees etc, the previously strong work ethic of the people was severely damaged, a problem that it appears everyone from bishops, community leaders, pastors, churches and families alike are still contending with today. Our staff members have consistently had to work through these high expectations of hand-outs, and through their skill and determination our programme has had considerable success in cracking this huge and destructive dependency culture. We continue to urge our team to remain crystal clear and devoted to the dream of asset-based development, even if this appears to achieve less in the short term.

Kyrgyzstan

I sense that when Christians in the UK pray for 'the persecuted church', they tend to have an image of brave (or maybe frightened) believers huddling in dark basements, quietly praising God and reading their bibles, and hoping that no-one will hear or discover them. Undoubtedly in some places this might be a fairly accurate picture. And pray for these, our precious brothers and sisters, we must.

But my friends in Kyrgyzstan lead a very different lifestyle. Kyrgyzstan is a country where Protestant Christians are formally regarded as followers of a 'non-traditional religion', i.e. a sect. Registration of their churches is only possible when (at the risk of them losing their jobs and a whole lot more) two hundred people sign to say they are members – a near impossibility in all places outside the capital. Orthodoxism is tolerated as 'the Russian's religion', but the dominant religion is Islam. Simply put, this comes in different forms, but much of it is best described as 'folk-Islam'; a cocktail of Muslim, witchcraft and local animist traditions. The word 'Baptist' is used as a swear word.

Kyrgyz believers regularly encounter the 'flash flood' or 'thunderstorm' forms of persecution that I mentioned earlier in this study. All may be quiet for weeks, but then if a neighbour, local authority representative or relative takes offence at something said or done, suddenly and without notice Christians can find themselves on the receiving end of exclusion, hostility or violence. Typical of the alienation issues they have to face is the refusal of authorities to let their deceased be buried in community graveyards (which are considered by the Moldo's or

179

Imam's to be Muslim), or the refusal of village elders to allow believers to enter the local shops or use public grazing lands for their sheep. Cases of violent attacks on Christians are all too frequent, as I have sadly witnessed for myself.

Into this environment come our *RaFa*-equipped churches, proclaiming the gospel of Jesus and intelligently serving the most vulnerable families in their communities. Rather than being huddled nervously in their proverbial basements, these churches are engaging with the very authorities that have mistrusted them so much, building relationship and trust, and demonstrating a commitment to serve those that the rest of their society rejects. These believers have become a significant means of reducing street homelessness, they provide training on health, nutrition and livelihoods, and they advocate for marginalised school children rejected by their own teachers. They restore access to clinics and hospitals for those who through the impact of alcoholism and drugs have lost their registration paperwork, and they provide development and employment services for the physically and mentally disabled, who were previously locked away in their homes through shame. They improve shelter, nutrition and community structures for the elderly, and are a means by which many families are being restored to loving healthy relationships.

Maybe we should change our mindset about the persecuted church!

Questions for Group Discussion

- Most would agree that the European Convention on Human Rights (1953) and the UK Human Rights Act (1998) have given us all a much stronger awareness of the need for justice and the opportunity of equality in our society.

- Share together some of the ways in which vulnerable people and little-understood minority groups in our country benefit from the protections and opportunities brought about from these Human Rights Acts. Think for example about their impact on central and local governments, upon our police and our courts. Think about the protection they offer to women against domestic violence, and about the non-acceptance of hateful discrimination that our society now aims to give to those of different ethnicity, disability and gender persuasion.

- Now share together some of the positive impacts that Health and Safety Acts have had on our society since the mid- to late-twentieth century.

- Is it true to say that our society is now better and more developed than it was twenty years ago?

- In what ways does our risk-averse culture deter us from pressing on into tough service for Jesus?

- Someone once said, *"'I know my rights' is almost always spoken with anger, and often by those who don't."* What do you feel when you hear someone argue, "I know my rights!"?
- What if anything have been the *negative* impacts of a greater Human Rights Awareness (HRA) on our psyche, world view, or culture?
- In what ways has it damaged our capacity to respond well to hardship and suffering? Has it (e.g.) instead given us another opportunity to issue blame, to avoid certain responsibilities, and provided an alternative to forgiveness and mercy? Is its goal restoration and reconciliation, or demand and punishment? Are 'Rights' without God like judgement without mercy?
- Has HRA given backbone or justification to a victim mentality, a grievance culture, or a glass half empty attitude?
- *Why* do we think the grass is always greener on the other side?
- How can we make sure we refuse to embrace a victim mentality?

Study Ten

Key Facilitators

The indispensable people who make things happen

Health Warning

"I have a cunning plan," as Baldrick said to Blackadder, slightly *too* many times.

We love new ideas, new formats, new titles, new 'movements', don't we. I've seen churches sell their proverbial soul to them. We hear what God is doing Colombia, or Nigeria, or Argentina, and how a certain model or way of doing things has been a means of heralding in a great revival or renewal. So we invite the pioneers of that movement to come and speak at our European conferences, and in great anticipation we all go home, abandon what we were doing and try to copy the format of what they've done. We experience an encouraging honeymoon of success, after which it peaks, and then we wonder why it doesn't have the same long term effect as it had in Colombia, or Nigeria, or Argentina. I've been round the block enough times now to have seen this happen time and time again. The Praise movement. The Charismatic movement. Home groups. Cell groups. Living in Community. Shepherding (or 'Heavy Shepherding' as its critics called it). The Toronto blessing. Missional Communities. *Raising Families.*

So this series comes with a health warning. Please don't sell your soul to *'Raising Families'*! It's the most enjoyable, fulfilling and effective initiative I've done in all my years with Samaritan's Purse, and it's true; the whole point of this book is so that the UK church can sit at the feet of our brothers and sisters in other lands, and humbly learn from them. But it's not the *formula* I want to see replicated, but the *spirit* of it; its *values*. It's not a project to be copied. In fact I really don't see it as a *project* at all. I can just about cope with it being called a *programme*, in that it has a model, a shape and a framework. But I'd rather it was known as a *process*: something that gradually, simply and naturally morphs into existence in each local context, as God blows His Spirit and favour all over it.

Because *"unless the LORD builds the house, the builders labour in vain. Unless the LORD watches over the city, the guards stand watch in vain. In vain you rise early and stay up late, toiling... for he grants sleep to those he loves"* (Psalm 127:1 NIV).

And I'm reminded of what Paul said about the Macedonians. *"And they exceeded our expectations: they gave themselves first of all to the Lord, and then by the will of God also to us."* (2 Corinthians 8:5 NIV).

So the well-being and success of *Raising Families*, and of almost any initiative really, is more about people than it is about cunning plans. It's about people who have given themselves to God, rather than to a system. People who have truly and gratefully placed themselves into God's hands, whether they are visible to the crowd or not, are always the key to the implementation of effective change.

I am amazed at how even some of the most dynamic organisations, with their extraordinary initiatives, ideas and marketing, still manage to mess up and waste a massive amount of resources, all because they don't maximise their most precious resource – people. In one sense, people is all *Raising Families* has. People as leaders, people as servants, people as examples, and people as mentors. If I had to select one word that most described the function of the key contributors to the *Raising Families* process, I would call these people facilitators.

And so this chapter looks at the roles of these key contributors of the *Raising Families* process. To those of you who fulfil these roles within the *Raising Families* process around the world, I salute you. I have gained much refreshment and encouragement from you; from your determination to humbly follow the Lord Jesus Christ, and to seek first *His* Kingdom.

The Biblical Rationale

The resurrected Jesus Christ, the Lamb of God who takes away the sin of the world (John 1:29), actually came and *breathed* on His disciples and said, *"Receive the Holy Spirit"* (John 20:22 NIV).

The Church was born!

Then Jesus' final instruction to the disciples, immediately before ascending into heaven, was to *"wait for the promise of the Father"*, and He told them that *"in a few days you will be baptised with the Holy Spirit"* (Acts 1:4-5 NIV).

The Church was equipped!

It was on the day of Pentecost that with the sound of a violent wind, what appeared to be tongues of fire separated and came to rest on each of the disciples. *"All of them were all filled with the Holy Spirit and began to speak in other tongues as the Spirit enabled them"* (Acts 2:2-4 NIV).

The Church was empowered!

It was *so* dynamic. Thousands came to Christ and were baptised, there was an abundance of signs and wonders, and a devoted community of believers were together, having all things in common, praising God and having favour with all the people.

But rapid growth and the interaction of people is never without its issues, and with ruthless honesty, and alongside many testimonies of the amazing moves of the Holy Spirit, the Acts of the Apostles also addresses the practical challenges they faced as they learned how to be the Community of the Redeemed. In the overseeing of these practical needs, we were about to be introduced to the role of the 'deacon'.

Among the key contributors in the *Raising Families* process are the *co-ordinators*, or facilitators. It is they who have the day to day responsibility to envision, train, equip and mentor a number of the Church Action Groups (CAGs), particularly working with the CAG leaders. We don't *call* them deacons, but when we train them and the CAG leaders, we often use the biblical teaching on deacons as our model.

The introduction of the role of deacons in the church came about following difficult discussions and disagreements between two groups of Jewish believers (Acts 6). In the daily distribution of food, some widows were allegedly being overlooked, and there was a groundswell of murmuring and complaint. It was down to the twelve disciples to sort this problem out, and to do so as soon as possible. This was the context for the statement they made to the gathered church.

"It would not be right for us to neglect the ministry of the word of God in order to wait on tables" (Acts 6:2 NIV). The time had come to spread the load of leadership responsibility, and to establish some good delegating processes. If they didn't do this, and do it quickly, then the murmurings could soon turn into something

nastier. The apostles probably recalled Moses reaching a similar crunch time (Exodus 18:17-23), when his father-in-law gave him a good talking to over the need for healthy delegation.

Whenever we commence our envisioning for *Raising Families*, we hear a lot of pastors saying similar things. 'My calling is to preach. That's the role of the pastor. That's what the church is here for. It would not be right for me to neglect the ministry of the word of God in order to serve the poor.' I do respect this view, to a degree, although I fear that when said in a small local context, it often produces quite a thin church, and can easily lead to dependency on one person rather than onto Christ. Developing a successful preaching centre is one thing, but it's a very different and more challenging thing to bring into existence a vibrant and interactive, worshipping and evangelising, community-connected resource that we could legitimately call a local church.

I once spent some time with one full-time pastor of a small church in Michigan, who for years had spent no less than thirty hours a week preparing his twenty minute Sunday morning talk. On the rare occasions when this level of investment of his time was impossible, he would torment himself with anxiety and guilt. The consistent end result was a beautifully crafted address, more like a work of art than a sermon, which was a great joy and privilege for me (and his congregation of thirty or so people) to listen to. But he inevitably had little time for anything or anyone else. And if I'm really honest, I think this huge investment of time preparing sermons probably gave my friend some seemingly justifiable protection from doing other tasks and forms of service that a small church leader could and should more realistically be undertaking.

I don't think that's what the apostles were saying in Acts 6. Theirs was a huge, pioneering, early-days, Spirit-led environment which needed just the lightest of organisational touches to stay on course; slight adjustments to the beds and banks that would enable the river to continue to flow. Demonstrating great trust in their new congregation and in the Spirit of God, they encouraged the church *"to choose seven men from among you who are known to be full of the Holy Spirit and wisdom. We will turn this responsibility over to them and will give our attention to prayer and the ministry of the word"* (Acts 6:3-4 NIV). And so deacons were formed in the Church.

The job description for deacons was to *"wait on tables"* (Acts 6:2 NIV). One would think, therefore, that the person spec would be something relevant to the task, like 'must know from which side to serve wine', 'should be experienced at feeding widows', and 'food hygiene certificate preferred'. However, for deacons in the early Church, the person specification was 'must be full of God's grace and power' (Acts 6:8), 'should be experienced in performing great wonders and signs' (Acts 6:8), and 'applicants with faces like angels preferred' (Acts 6:15).

What I'm saying is this. The bible never undermines or puts into second place the practical works of service in the church. They were of no lesser importance than the ministry of prayer and the ministry of the word. The *functions* might have been different, but all those who served, in whatever capacity, were required to be filled with the Holy Spirit. This is well summed up in Romans 12:3-8, where Paul says that whatever our gifts and function, we all belong to one another. As if to illustrate his point, when giving examples of some of the different gifts he had in mind, it is noticeable that Paul listed 'serving' before 'teaching', and that he mentioned 'encouraging' before he mentions 'leading'.

Paul commended Phoebe, a deacon of the church in Cenchreae. He spoke highly of her, and urged the believers in Rome to receive and support her (Romans 16:1). When bringing his initial greeting to the church in Philippi, he specifically mentioned the overseers and the deacons together (Philippians 1:1). And after outlining the requirements for the office of overseers to Timothy, he immediately went on discuss deacons *"in the same way"* (1 Timothy 3:8 NIV), going on to say that those who have served well *"gain an excellent standing and great assurance in their faith in Christ Jesus"* (I Timothy 3:13 NIV).

Not everyone was eligible to become a deacon. Deacons were to be *"worthy of respect, sincere, not indulging in much wine, and not pursuing dishonest gain"*. They were to *"keep hold of the deep truths of the faith with a clear conscience"*. Before they served as deacons, they were first to be tested. They were to be faithful to their wife, and must manage their children and their household well. The women deacons (or possibly this referred to deacons' wives) were also to be *"worthy of respect, not malicious talkers but temperate and trustworthy in everything"* (I Timothy 3:8-12 NIV).

The Raising Families Context

Before we look at how these deacon-like coordinators or facilitators function, let's look at the role of those who hold overall leadership responsibility within the *RaFa* process.

RaFa Country Directors

These are the men and women who have overall responsibility for *Raising Families* in their country. Theirs is a full-time salaried role, although in several cases they also hold the office of senior pastor or leader in their own church, and some are also directors of NGOs that undertake other like-minded programmes as well.

I work very closely with each Country Director. They effectively become my gateway into hundreds of churches in their own nations. Their role is to ensure that the programme maintains its spiritual, relational and practical focus and momentum, to look back and evaluate, and to look ahead so that it grows and reaches its goals. Each of them loves their nation and their community, and every one of them has a genuine respect for those in positions of authority within it. The same goes for the Church; they love it and sincerely respect those whom God has raised up to lead it, be it nationally or locally. God has equipped all of these men and women with strong leadership gifts, and although every one of them leads in their own unique style, one can clearly detect in each of them a strong understanding of how their communities work, the capacity to teach clearly, to address difficult issues, and to humbly serve the poorest in their communities.

National Denominational Church Leaders

We have found through our research that when national and regional church leaders understand and are excited about the *Raising Families* programme, the Church Action Groups are more likely to grow stronger and to multiply. We are always encouraged when national church leaders not only attend key *RaFa* events (such as launch events and graduations), but also maintain an active interest in the programme's development at every stage. The Anglican Archbishops of both Rwanda and Uganda have even travelled to the UK for the specific purpose of promoting the programme and strengthening relationships within it.

We have found that the most effective *RaFa* programmes are those where the senior church leadership teams in the region fully and actively promote it. They might not have the same hands-on role as other practitioners, but neither are they aloof or separate from it. They attend key trainings, they check on progress, they advise against error and imbalance. And they have a deep respect for the work of the Regional Co-ordinators and Church Action Group Leaders.

Community Leaders

Various prestigious community awards have been won by our teams as a result of local authority and social service teams appreciating the work of *Raising Families*. Such people regularly attend our trainings and ceremonies in every one of the countries we work in. With their desperately tight budgets and their restrictive political complexities, many of them tell us (albeit informally) that they would love to have seen even half the outcomes our churches see. But their support is also invaluable to the programme, and is a demonstration to the poorest rural communities that what they have achieved is being recognised in places of influence.

Regional Co-ordinators

As with our Country Directors, the Regional (or Diocesan, or Zone) Co-ordinators are also paid employees of the programme. In fact, salaries and the travel expenses of the staff members make up over 90% of the *RaFa* budgets. The number of Co-ordinators varies, depending on the size of the programme and the accessibility of the locations they are committed to. In Africa the regional co-ordinators usually travel by motor bike, but in Central Asia, with its harsh winters, mountainous terrain and thin spread of churches, travel is much more complex, requiring long bus journeys, or hitching a lift on a coal truck, or sometimes even taking a domestic flight to get to some locations. But typically, each regional co-ordinator is responsible for the training and mentoring of between twenty and fifty local Church Action Groups.

Some, but not all, are pastors. Some, but not all, have had some training in theology. Almost all have had good previous experience in some form of community development. They are trainers, enablers, mentors, coaches, equippers and, as we have emphasised throughout this study, they are facilitators. They love God, the Word of God, and the Church. They understand how communities work. They understand the components and processes of change. They understand facilitation, empowerment, monitoring and the significance of local ownership. Consequently, they will usually ask more questions than they give answers. They are ready to give the power away rather than to hold onto it for their own gain.

Church Action Group Leaders

Only occasionally is this role taken by the local church pastor. Typically the CAG leader is one of the key activists in the church.

None of them are paid. Often this is the first time they have had a recognised leadership role either in their church or their community, but I have seen some wonderful CAG leaders at work. Some are in their early twenties, and others are in their seventies. I would estimate that around the world there is a more or less an equal mix of men and women.

I've watched them worship, pray and train. I have seen them leading by example when it comes to hard work and serving the poor in the dirtiest of environments, and I've seen the sparkle in their eyes as they testify to what God has done with them all. They don't *do* all the work that is planned and coordinated (e.g. they often appoint an administrator/report writer and a treasurer from within the CAG), but they play an active role in it, and ensure that it gets done. I recall hardly ever seeing CAG leaders who glory in their role. These are simple community members, often uneducated and sometimes illiterate, who model servant leadership in their local environment. Their pastors are clearly very proud of them.

Despite their lack of formal education, they need the capacity to teach others, and to 'bed in' the training they receive from the regional co-ordinators when back in their own village. They will need to oversee the effective functioning of a savings and loans group, the keeping of records of their activities, and monitoring their results. There are more than 1,800 such volunteers fulfilling this function around the world today.

Testimonies from Raising Families Practitioners

RaFa Country Directors

Revealing God's Love

"My vision and my role is to see strong churches reaching out holistically into their Muslim communities, bringing transformation and revealing God's love to people. We do it through training, facilitating and establishing social ministries in churches. We provide support and mentor them until they run this ministry by themselves.

Questions, questions, and more questions. This is one of the key elements of our work. We ask a lot of questions, and then listen carefully. Why? Because the questions help to identify the potential of the CAG, how far they want to go in partnership with us and how sustainable the CAG will be after we finish our programme with them". *RaFa National Director, Kyrgyzstan.*

Ensuring Good Coordination

"My roles and responsibilities include managing, planning, coordination and supervising. I recruit, train, mentor and supervise staff to fill different positions within the programme. I conduct quarterly reviews with staff to ensure that planned results are being attained, and I make adjustments to realign activities that do not seem to be leading to attainment of the intended results. I also build partnerships with denominational church leaders so as to ensure good coordination through information sharing, training and joint field visits. This helps us all to learn about programme achievements and challenges, and so forge the best way forward." *RaFa National Programme Manager, Uganda.*

Empowering the Church

"I oversee our work which is through local churches in Swaziland. I see my role as helping to bring about transformed rural communities through empowering the church and its leaders to recognise and act in their God given mandate to help drive economic, social and spiritual empowerment in their communities, thus alleviating and mitigating poverty." *RaFa National Programme Director, Swaziland.*

Good and Godly Leadership

"My role is to coordinate and supervise all activities relating to *RaFa*, to provide leadership to our area coordinators, zone leaders and CAGs. I seek to provide good and Godly leadership to the team, coaching and motivating them to ministry effectiveness. I manage the affairs of *RaFa* Zambia Programme and provide direction for the expansion and growth of the programme. I facilitate in the implementation of the policies, plans, aims and objectives as required by our funders, Samaritan's Purse. I am the chief spokesperson of the *RaFa* Zambia programme, and report, review and evaluate the performance of *RaFa* Zambia as enshrined in the Memorandum of Understanding. I look for growth opportunities for the programme and liaise with cooperating partners." *RaFa National Director, Zambia.*

Community Leaders

Local authority support and recognition

"*Raising Families* is a very good programme which needs and deserves the support of all of us. Wherever families are breaking up the community itself ceases to develop, because you cannot develop without unity. *Raising Families* will help us meet some of the challenges we have been encountering in our community, such as gender based violence, and divorce, which is a national challenge. But with the coming of this programme I am pretty sure that such problems will be mitigated and will be lessened in our community.

As a government, and as a local authority, we cannot do without the support of the church. The church remains an integral part of development, both at community and at national level, and we cannot do without your support. The *Raising Families* initiative is one that can supplement government's efforts in ensuring that we raise healthy communities and that we take development to every part of our community. So we shall continue to support you and as you work within our community and in the other communities where you work." *Area Councillor, Municipal Council, Mapalo, Ndola Central Constituency, Zambia.*

Most Progressive Young Farmer Award

Evarist was left as an orphan at 17 when his mother died, and lived alone in a straw-roof house with nothing to eat and nothing to do. He decided to head east and seek work, becoming a house boy doing domestic work for nine months before returning with a small gift from his employers. A local health centre sold him some carrot seeds and he did his best by cultivating the carrots on the small plot of land left by his mother. This he did for some time, getting married and starting a family, but not having enough to feed them.

"Then Didasienne (*RaFa's Regional Coordinator*) brought us some training. At its core it was about total transformation; spiritual, social and welfare transformation." As a result the local church (of which Evarist was by now a member) started a savings group, with twenty families selected due to their vulnerability and poverty. Inspired and motivated to reinvest his earnings, he sold his latest carrot crop for 7,000 RWF and, together with a loan from the *RaFa* savings group, he bought a piglet. Evarist spoke of the rapid progression of those who had committed to the CAG savings and loans group. "Our twenty families save just 50 RWF each week, and loan from the scheme to buy vegetables to sell.

Reinvesting the profits, they move on to purchasing livestock. The loans are repaid at 10% interest per month."

Before the training, Evarist's family ate once a day, with a poor diet, and struggled to pay for medical insurance and keep a roof over their heads. Evarist contracted to tend gardens in order to top up his savings. Gradually he cultivated more crops, borrowing or hiring other people's gardens. He eagerly tuned into radio programmes that would give him further training on the effective cultivating and selling of his crops. Now he is able to harvest 10 x 100kg sacks of carrots, has sold nine pigs, and has bought land to expand his vegetable crop, which now brings in 800,000 RWF. He has branched out into potatoes, maize, beans and an onion nursery, and has built a large new house, using his original home to house his chickens.

But this is not merely a testimony of one man's growing prosperity. Evarist shares his produce with his neighbours, and invests a lot of time into training others, not regarding them as competitors but as neighbours in need. "Five of the families I've trained are doing really well," he admits coyly, "and at least another twenty have come, sometimes from a distance, to see how we do things." He has given permanent employment to seven people.

"The church teaches us how to love Jesus and how to live well, free from poverty" he says. "I used to be blind to these things, and without the *RaFa* training I would still be sowing a handful of carrots and struggling to provide for my family."

The day I visited Evarist, I was not his only guest. A smart young man had been listening to Evarist's story, and stepped forward to introduce himself. Jean-Paul was the local authority Executive Secretary for Community Development. "We recognise that Evarist is a glowing example of what is possible in the community," he told us. "Many others come to him for training, and we are delighted to award him the title of Most Progressive Young Farmer." Jean-Paul continued to travel with us all day and, when we were all presented to one of the host churches later in the day, he stood to address the church. My fears that his speech would be self-congratulatory local authority spin were completely unfounded. "It is wonderful to see the gospel being practised so openly in the community. Never forget that faith without works is dead," he said.

Encouragement from the Tribal Chief

Our team in Swaziland started working in one particular region where the community was quite resistant to the messages. Our team was ready to end the envisioning process and move on, when the regional Chief stood up and told the people that the *RaFa* team were *his* guests, and that the people must listen to them very carefully. "We want to work with these people", he said.

After addressing the gathering the chief instructed the fifteen church pastors who had attended to affirm their commitment to the programme. The pastors who had failed to turn up were then fined by the Chief one goat each for not responding to his "royal command"! A total of seventeen pastors are still on the programme, and the area's wellbeing has improved tremendously. Seven cult churches have repented and changed their beliefs after the pastors' trainings, and to date there have been 171 conversions in these churches. All the 17 churches are vibrant and the church members are growing steadily. Perhaps the most significant thing that has impacted this region is the unexpectedly high commitment of the church volunteers. Some of the greatest progress has been made in this community with HIV interventions, referrals to specialised help, psychosocial support and the care of orphans and vulnerable children (OVC). 648 people have been trained on HIV, 1,798 people have been tested for HIV, 428 OVC are receiving psychosocial support, and 238 young people have been trained in basic life skills and gardening. 33 child-headed homes now have adult foster parents and 22 families have moved from the formal category of 'very vulnerable' to 'not vulnerable at all'.

Regional Co-ordinators

Strong and Courageous

"I see my role as helping churches to establish and develop social ministry in their communities. We serve mainly in Muslim villages and towns where the church is not accepted and is persecuted, and my task is to make the church strong and courageous to reach unsaved souls through the care of poor and destitute people." *Regional Co-ordinator, Kyrgyzstan.*

Supporting the CAGs

"My role is to lead the zone Leaders, CAGs and to coordinate the programme in the assigned churches. This involves leading church leaders in the implementation of the programme, gathering and collating data from the churches and target families, implementing the action plan according to the agreed standard and deadlines. I report to and update the Assistant Manager and Programme Manager on outputs and outcomes. I have regular contact with the church leaders, CAGs and target families on all programme-related matters, and support the CAGs through training in key development sectors. I ensure the effective preparation and delivery of all programme events and meetings, and production of all necessary documentations. I track our activities and undertake ongoing evaluation of programme activity." *Area Co-ordinator, Zambia.*

Trainer of Trainers

"In *Raising Families*, I see my role as a trainer of trainers, a mentor and a change agent within the community. During the

training I use a lot of discussions and experience sharing to promote learning amongst learners. I also use questions to ensure learning is going on well. After training the church leaders, I follow up all those who attended the training to ensure they are putting into practice what they have learnt. Those who missed important points or information are coached outside of the class. Trainees who are slow at grasping information are coached individually. I do all this to ensure the proper running of the programme. I compile monthly reports and send them to the National Programme Director. As a Regional Coordinator I am responsible to ensure that the church leaders take up the mantel of Jesus Christ in caring for and standing with those in need."
Regional Coordinator, Uganda.

Church Action Group Leaders

Reconcilers and restorers

"My role and the role of our CAG is to help people who have been rejected by society, who have completely lost hope in this life. If we as a church do not show them God and His infinite love, then what should these people hope for in this life and in eternity? Our task is to make them reconcile with Him and with God's help restore their human dignity." *CAG leader in Central Asia.*

Become a light to this world

"My vision as a Christian in my Muslim village is to establish good collaboration of the church with state structures for the benefit of the community. Today we see that through our ministry to children with disabilities and assistance to their parents, people in the village have become different. They became kinder, and they began to understand that we ourselves can change the lives of the most vulnerable people for the better. Become a light to this world and protect the dispossessed; this is the vision and purpose of God's church." *CAG leader in Central Asia.*

Change Agents

"We see our CAG leaders (and members) as change agents working to bring about spiritual, social and economic transformation in the lives of vulnerable families. We have made sure they are trained and mentored in topics like children discipleship, saving, livelihood, health, hygiene and sanitation and agronomic practices." *CAG leader in Uganda.*

Guide and Support

"My role is to mobilise all the Church Action Group (CAG) members in my church to attend different trainings, and to move into the community as a team to proclaim and demonstrate the gospel to those in need. I provide leadership to the members of my congregation, training the CAGs in various livelihoods and ministry trainings. I'm also involved in the daily running of the group activities and record-keeping of the group's activities. I guide and support the CAG members to visit the vulnerable people within our community in order that they can offer compassionate care to them and share the gospel with such families." *CAG leader in Uganda.*

Questions for Group Discussion

- Which 'movements of God' or 'revival times' have you personally experienced since becoming a Christian? How long did they last, and what happened to them?

- Which people have mentored, influenced and inspired you most to follow Jesus more? Name them by name, briefly tell the group about them, and why they were such a positive influence to you.

- Individually write down the five roles in your church (e.g. pastor, cleaner, worship leader etc) that you think are the most 'key' to its success. Now all share them with each other, and through consensus agree the five primary roles that collectively your group feels are most crucial.

- However their role is described, how seriously is the office of 'deacon' taken in your church?

- If a local authority official came to speak to your church, what would she/he most likely say were the main contributions your church is making to the community?

- If your church was to start a *"Raising Families"* type programme, who do you think would make good CAG members and why, and who would you like to see *leading* this team?
- What are the skills a good facilitator needs to use, and what are their goals?
- Why will a good facilitator often ask more questions than she/he gives answers?

Study Eleven

Measuring Impact

Understanding monitoring, evaluation and learning

How Do We Know?

The Continuous Improvement Process (CIP) is the ongoing effort to improve products, services or processes. These efforts can be incremental over time, or be achieved through sudden breakthrough moments.

Basically it is an approach to quality management. When it is inappropriately forced upon workers by anxious managers who are a) desperate for higher productivity whilst b) being unprepared to commit to further investment, it can be very stressful. Just how many times can I *re*-double my efforts which, by my calculation, already equates to four times my original effort? To be honest, my natural response to this unrealistic and externally imposed 'turning of the screw' is to think (and sometimes to say), "You are just never quite satisfied, are you?"

However, where we are able to voluntarily and intelligently resolve to apply CIP to ourselves, we would probably all applaud the basic concept of improvement, and the idea of it being a lifestyle rather than a random or one-off occasion. Paul expressed it superbly to the Philippians, when he outlined his determination to count everything else as loss for the sake of gaining Christ and being found in Him. For him this was not a single decision or an already reached goal, but a direction of travel.

"I do not regard myself as having laid hold of it yet; but one thing I do: forgetting what lies behind and reaching forward to what lies ahead, I press on toward the goal for the prize of the upward call of God in Christ Jesus." (Philippians 3:13-14 NASB).

But whatever the context of our aim to improve (e.g. our skills, our character, our marriage etc), how do we know whether or not we *have* actually improved? Without measuring, we are speculating.

I have a friend who worked for many months at a time doing relief and development work in a tiny corner of a small country in the vast continent of Africa. He would return to the West for a rest, only to be asked ridiculously sweeping questions like, "How's Africa?"! Similarly, "How's the church?" is a question that local church leaders have had to field for years.

On the basis of the church being made up of people, and therefore assuming the question didn't relate to dry rot or a damp course, when I was a local church pastor I would reply, "Well some are rejoicing, some are hurting; some are doing really well, and some are doing not so well."

But let's be honest. Typically, the church has not been great at *measuring* its progress, particularly in qualitative terms. Too many pastors are content to measure their current state of affairs by merely reporting that "God is greatly blessing us" (i.e. a couple of families have left the church down the road and joined ours), or "We are going through a time of pruning" (i.e. a couple of families from our church have left and gone to the one down the road). Come on, Church! Surely we can do better than that!

The Biblical Rationale

The bible is full of measurements.

Talents, mina, shekel, pim, beka and gerah. These are all weights. Cubit, span and handbreadth are measures of length, and cor, homer, ephah, seah, omer, cab, (dry) and bath, hin and log (liquid) are measurements of capacity. *"An omer is one-tenth of an ephah"* (Exodus 16:36) is surely one of the most random verses of scripture! More than once, cheekily, I have been tempted to 'encourage' someone with that scripture!

Very often the measuring we read of in the bible was for good and wholesome, or at least necessary, reasons.

It ensured fairness (Exodus 16:18 NIV – *"And when they measured [the manna] by the omer, the one who gathered much did not have too much, and the one who gathered little did not have too little. Everyone had gathered just as much as they needed"*), particularly fairness towards the poor (Amos 8:4-5). And it ensured accuracy and honesty (Duet 25:13-16, Proverbs 20:10).

It was used in the context of town and country planning (Numbers 35:1-5 NIV – *"Outside the town, measure two thousand cubits on the east side, two thousand on the south side, two thousand on the west and two thousand on the north, with the town in the centre. They will have this area as pastureland for the towns."*), and especially and specifically for the building of the temple (1 Kings 5-7).

Not only were measurements of the physical temple crucial, but a lot of attention was also given to measurements in prophecies concerning the temple. Ezekiel was told to *"look carefully and listen closely"* to the vision of the temple. He then recorded the measurements of at least forty-four different aspects of the temple (Ezekiel 40-44). Angels even argued over the value of measuring Jerusalem (Zechariah 2:1-5), and they were still measuring both the temple and the city of Jerusalem in Revelation (Rev 11:1-2, Rev 21:15-17).

But should we *always* measure *everything* related to God and His Kingdom? Are there limits to what we should measure and boundaries for what we should not? From a further look into the

211

scriptures, the answer is clearly yes. Yes, there are limits and yes, there are times when it is downright wrong.

Firstly, consider God's overwhelming abundance towards us. Can it be measured? Genesis 41:49 (NIV) tells us that *"Joseph stored up huge quantities of grain, like the sand of the sea; it was so much that he stopped keeping records because it was beyond measure."* In I Kings 4:29 (NIV), *"God gave Solomon wisdom and very great insight, and a breadth of understanding as measureless as the sand on the seashore."* Although having said that, the writer still had a go, immediately quantifying the number of proverbs and songs that Solomon wrote (1 Kings 4:32)!

In Job 11:7-9 (NIV) we are reminded of the mysteries and the limits of the Almighty, that *"their measure is longer than the earth and wider than the sea."*

And Isaiah asks, *"Who has measured the waters in the hollow of his hand, or with the breadth of his hand marked off the heavens? Who has held the dust of the earth in a basket, or weighed the mountains on the scales and the hills in a balance? Who can fathom the Spirit of the LORD, or instruct the LORD as his counsellor? Surely the nations are like a drop in a bucket; they are regarded as dust on the scales; he weighs the islands as though they were fine dust"* (Isaiah 40:12-15 NIV).

Through Jeremiah, the Lord throws out a challenge to our monitoring capacity. *"Only if the heavens above can be measured*

and the foundations of the earth below be searched out will I
reject all the descendants of Israel because of all they have done"
(Jeremiah 31:37 NIV). He goes on to say, *"I will make the*
descendants of David my servant and the Levites who minister
before me as countless as the stars in the sky and as measureless
as the sand on the seashore" (Jeremiah 33:22 NIV).

However, there are many mentions of God commissioning, and of
people conducting a census in the Old Testament. *"The Lord will*
write a register of the peoples: This one was born in Zion" (Psalm
87:6 NIV). And being counted in a census was one of the first
experiences Jesus had as a baby.

And when He was an adult, Jesus had some very interesting things
to say about measuring and monitoring.

Of the Spirit of God He told us that try as we might, we would
never be able to fully capture Him and His work. *"The wind blows*
wherever it pleases. You hear its sound, but you cannot tell where
it comes from or where it is going. So it is with everyone born of
the Spirit" (John 3:8 NIV), and, *"God gives the Spirit without limit"*
(John 3:34 NIV).

But when it came to the joy of the Lord, Jesus said (in John 17:13
NIV) *"I am coming to you now, but I say these things while I am*
still in the world, so that they may have the full measure of my joy
within them".

And Jesus clearly monitors and measures other aspects of life too, such as judgement and generosity. He told us that *"in the same way you judge others, you will be judged, and with the measure you use, it will be measured to you"* (Matthew 7:2 NIV). He warned us in Mark 4:24 (NIV) that *"the measure you use, it will be measured to you—and even more"*. Again in Luke 6:38 (NIV) Jesus said, *"Give, and it will be given to you. A good measure, pressed down, shaken together and running over, will be poured into your lap. For with the measure you use, it will be measured to you."*

Like Jesus, Paul also spoke in terms of a "full" or a "whole" measure, saying in Romans 15:29 (NIV), *"I know that when I come to you, I will come in the full measure of the blessing of Christ."* And similarly in Ephesians 3:19 (NIV), he prayed, *"that you may be filled to the measure of all the fullness of God."* And again in Ephesians 4:13 (NIV) Paul said that the five-fold leadership ministries to the church were given for the purpose of reaching *"unity in the faith and in the knowledge of the Son of God and becoming mature, attaining to the whole measure of the fullness of Christ."*

Regarding the use of prophecy, Paul urges the church to *"weigh carefully what is said"* (1 Corinthians 14:29 NIV). For years I heard this taught in the quite stark context of weighing whether it was 'right' or 'wrong'; i.e. from God or from the enemy. Although this might be implied in other scriptures (e.g. 2 Peter 2:1), here Paul simply asks us to *weigh* the prophecy, i.e. to put it on the scales, and to evaluate whether this is to be received as an encouraging word from God merely for today, or whether it has more foundational implications for the way we are to lead and direct our lives from here on in. Paul also urged the church to *"eagerly desire the greater gifts"* (1 Corinthians 12:31 NIV), the implication being that some gifts are more significant than others.

But Paul stopped at seeking to measure himself against others. In 2 Corinthians 10:12 (NIV) he said, *"We do not dare to classify or compare ourselves with some who commend themselves. When they measure themselves by themselves and compare themselves with themselves, they are not wise."*

And this was exactly what made God so angry with David in 1 Chronicles 21, back in the Old Testament. We read that David stirred up the anger of God by counting the fighting men of Israel (I Chronicles 21:1-7). Why was God angry with David? Many commentaries suggest that it was because David was trusting in his army rather than in God, and that was probably true. However, Got Questions Ministries offers an interesting and more specific thought as to the reason for God's anger, relating to ownership:

"In those times, a man only had the right to count or number what belonged to him. Israel did not belong to David; Israel belonged to God. In Exodus 30:12 God told Moses, "When you take a census of the Israelites to count them, each one must pay the LORD a ransom for his life at the time he is counted. Then no plague will

come on them when you number them." It was up to God to command a census, and if David counted he should only do it at God's command, receiving a ransom to "atone" for the counting. This is why God was angry again with Israel and is also why David was "conscience-stricken" after he counted Israel. David knew it was wrong and begged God to take away the guilt of his sin (2 Samuel 24:10)." [26]

So in conclusion I would suggest that monitoring is usually necessary for the good order of society, and for developing a good sense of the state of things, even the state of the local church, but that most importantly, God Himself will never be boxed in or controlled by numbers. That which man controls and is responsible for will probably benefit from a good degree of healthy monitoring and measurement, but that which belongs to God should never been taken, calculated or considered to be owned, possessed, controlled or limited by human effort and calculation. As is recorded in Matthew (22:21 NASB), Mark (12:17 NASB) and Luke (20:25 NASB), Jesus said, *"Then render to Caesar the things that are Caesar's; and to God the things that are God's."*

The Raising Families Context

---

[26] https://www.gotquestions.org/David-census.html

So in the context of *Raising Families*, how do we interpret all this practically?

From the outset, let me say that it is in no way our intention to turn churches into NGOs. Although some of their practices and activities might be similar and overlap, their ultimate function and purpose is quite different. However, in providing a service which envisions and equips the local church to become the facilitators of change in their communities, we do see the clear need to collect, analyse and utilise data in order to credibly monitor (*what* was achieved), evaluate (*how* it was achieved), learn from and report the results of our work.

As *practitioners*, this is to ensure we are doing the right things, and to see what worked well and why, and what could be improved upon and how. As *funding partners*, it enables us to ensure we are delivering what we are funded to do, and to report back to our donors so that they can test the value they have had for their money. As *learners*, or as *disciples*, it enables us to live transparently and accountably before God and one another, and not to hide behind opaque and religious assumptions. And for *academics* and *students*, it enables proper research and analysis to be done on the basis of quantifiable and qualitative evidence.

Using a relatively simple Lot Quality Assurance Sampling (LQAS) methodology, we equip and support our partners to undertake a baseline survey at the start of their programme, which firstly looks at matters relating to target *families* and

- Their livelihoods (e.g. the sources of family income, access to bank accounts, involvement in savings schemes etc)
- Their health (e.g. access to health services, food security and nutrition)
- Their education (e.g. enrolment, attendance and progress at school)
- Their shelter (the adequacy, humidity and safety of the home), and
- Their protection (issues surrounding abuse, neglect, and levels of care).

Secondly, we also do similar surveys to monitor the impact of the programme on the *church* (e.g. looking at its growth, understanding and levels of commitment to its community) and then thirdly with the *community* itself, monitoring the way the community perceives the church. Presently we also collate the numbers of people who are evidenced as having come to Christ for the first time, i.e. new Christians. But *should* we, or is this getting close to the holy ground that some of the scriptures used above refer to as God's business and not ours? Even within our organisation this is still being debated, and we would be grateful for your prayers and the wisdom of your comments on this matter.

Then after eighteen months (midpoint), and again at the end of each three year programme, we go through exactly the same process again. In this way growth and transformation in the church and the families can be reliably measured, the programme evaluated and the lessons learned.

So, for example, by monitoring we know that through the *Raising Families* programme in Swaziland (May 2012-April 2015) there was a:

- 67% growth in the number of target families whose children are progressing well in school (baseline 36%; endpoint 60%)
- 170% growth in the number of target families whose children are safe from abuse, neglect or exploitation (baseline 23%; endpoint 62%)
- 200% growth in the number of target families whose children have nutritious food at all times of the year (baseline 23%; endpoint 69%)
- 466% growth in the numbers of the population who perceive the church to be actively caring for vulnerable families in the community (baseline 12%; endpoint 68%).

Similarly, we know that through the *Raising Families* programme in Rwanda (April 2013-March 2016) there was a:

- 51% growth in the number of target families whose children are safe from abuse, neglect or exploitation (baseline 63%; endpoint 95%)

- 98% growth in the number of target families whose children have access to health services (baseline 43%; endpoint 85%)
- 215% growth in the number of target families that are saving regularly (baseline 13%; endpoint 41%)
- And that 2,732 members of the target families came to Christ.

And we know that through the *Raising Families* programme in Kyrgyzstan (July 2013-June 2016) there was a:

- 547% growth in the number of target families who have access to health services (baseline 15%; endpoint 97%)
- 600% growth in the number of target families who have adequate, dry and safe shelter (baseline 10%; endpoint 70%)
- 1500% growth in the number of target families that have sufficient and nutritious food at all times of the year (baseline 6%; endpoint 96%)
- And that 170 members of the target families came to Christ.

We also undertake a regular post-programme analysis (called a CIDOS review) which looks at the long term *Change* and *Impact* of our work, reviews the programme *Design*, the capacity of the implementing *Organisation*, and the *Sustainability* of *RaFa* in the years *after* training and support had finished.

This research has not only given us evidence and confidence that the programme is sustainable and naturally multiplies, but has also taught us valuable lessons such as a) the need to fully engage senior church leaders at the start and continuously throughout the programme, b) the need to start livelihoods training as early as possible in the three year process, and c) that the final year of the programme has to actively and intentionally ensure that families can not only stand on their own feet, but also that they have the vision and the skills to go on to equip other families in similar ways.

The measuring of our programme therefore qualifies us to give an account, it empowers us to plan, it allows us to adjust, it validates us to grow, and it enables us to rejoice. But to God be all the glory always. We stand on holy ground.

Testimonies from Raising Families Practitioners

God of Order

"Since we did not track changes in our work with families, very often our ministry was spontaneous. We jumped from one problem to another without resolving the former one. Because of this we were not effective, and were more responsive to current problems rather than bringing about any long-term changes. At that time I could not understand why we needed to monitor and evaluate everything. After all, I reasoned, God sees everything and knows everything that we do, so why should we keep notes?

However, after the M&E training we began to understand that our God is God of order. After monitoring and analysing our ministry we could see the weaknesses of our work and began to change things accordingly. I am very grateful for this knowledge on monitoring and evaluation as it has raised our ministry to a different, more effective level, and has given us an understanding of how to help families more effectively." *CAG leader, Kyrgyzstan.*

Writing Everything Down

"The hardest part of our ministry to poor families was getting used to writing everything down. We found reporting to be very difficult, until we saw the benefits to be gained from it. Through the recording, measuring and reporting of our work it became clear that we help families a lot more than we ever realised. When we began to monitor everything, we saw all the encouraging results of our ministry, and this gave us new motivation to move on." *CAG leader, Kyrgyzstan.*

The Importance of Planning

"Before, I did not plan anything and did not even know why we needed to. I reasoned that our God Himself moves wherever He wants and we need just follow Him. This is obviously true, but after the training on monitoring and evaluation, I also realised how important it is to record and plan everything. I began by planning and monitoring each day, week and month, not only for our work with poor families, but also for our ministry in the church. As a result, God's order came into my life and ministry, and I began to clearly see what I had achieved, and what I had missed. For example, I realised that I had too often concentrated on a humanitarian approach to ministry, because this addressed the obvious needs in front of us, but I had missed the more holistic, relational needs of people that were not so immediately obvious. Addressing these aspects of life has opened up new prospects for the future of the work and for these families." *Local church pastor, Kyrgyzstan.*

Individual Support Plans

"For several years our church has been supporting vulnerable families, but we never recorded anything as though it was not important. After the Monitoring and Evaluation training we started personal folders for each family, and soon we began to see the results of our work. Through this we realised we were doing so much *for* the families without them actively participating towards their own development. Now, together *with* these families, we develop individual plans as to how they can overcome the crises in their lives, and we now monitor progress together with families. Thanks to this monitoring, many families realised that it was actually *them* that needed to take responsibility to change and emerge from poverty." *Pastor's wife and CAG leader, Kyrgyzstan.*

Questions for Group Discussion

- 'Without measuring we are speculating'. Discuss the consequences of relying on speculation.
- What do we measure in our church, and in what ways are we speculating?
- *Why* do we measure? Is it primarily because external stakeholders (e.g. an auditor, the church denominational headquarters etc) require us to, or is it to enable our learning and growth?
- What (in the context of our church) could be helpfully measured?
- "As learners, or as disciples, measuring enables us to live transparently and accountably before God and one another, and not to hide behind opaque and religious assumptions." But are there pitfalls? What are the limitations? Do we want to measure *everything*? How can we learn the lessons of accountability without creating a judgemental, never satisfied, performance-based culture?

Study Twelve

Sustainability and Multiplication

Ensuring continued strength and growth

Inspire a Generation

This was the strapline at the heart of the pitch that won the bid by the British Olympic Association in 2005. It was the message that was plastered all over the Olympic Park in Stratford during that glorious period in July and August 2012. It was a proud legacy boast that the London Olympics could do something no other previous Games had achieved. But before long it became a millstone for all involved.

Only three of the 26 Olympic sports saw significant increases in the number of people playing in Britain in the three years following London 2012, by which time much of the £1bn in funding had gone to waste.

What resonated most with the International Olympic Committee and the UK as a whole was the "Singapore promise" of leaving behind a legacy of a fitter, healthier nation and transforming the lives of young people, together with regenerating a patch of east London and underlining the value of public investment in elite sport.

There were plenty of people, even then, who argued that investing £9.3bn in a major sporting event was not the most effective way to transform the fabric of grassroots sport in the UK. But the seductive vision from Lord Coe and the then prime minister, Tony Blair, was that hosting the Games could provide a glorious one-off corrective that in addition to regeneration in London and economic benefits for Britain could transform the attitude to sport in Whitehall and beyond.[27]

Sustainability has also long been the aim of those committed to intelligent community development, but it is still not easy to achieve. As the successor to the Millennium Development Goals, the UN-initiated Sustainable Development Goals (officially known as "Transforming our world: the 2030 agenda for Sustainable Development") is a set of seventeen goals consisting of 169 targets. They cover complex issues such as addressing poverty and hunger, improving health and education, making cities more sustainable, combating climate change, and protecting oceans and forests. It's a massive challenge. In order for the SDGs to succeed, each and every country must translate the goals into national legislation, develop a plan of action, allocate a budget, and openly search for partners. Poorer countries will need the support of richer countries, and coordination at an international level will be crucial. But will politicians be interested in tough and

---

[27] https://www.theguardian.com/sport/blog/2015/jul/05/olympic-legacy-failure-london-2012-message-millstone

expensive fifteen year plans, or fifty year plans, over and against a more self-absorbed approach of maintaining their popularity and therefore their power in the coming months?

And as for the church; well surely any church that has a prophetic edge will be as much 'future-orientated' as 'present-orientated', i.e. planting, building, discipling and mentoring towards a better future for its society as well as for itself. Although God sometimes chooses to raise up a movement or a local church for a short period of time, typically the dynamic church will recognise that it is a living organism. As such, whilst it will always seek to be faithful to the eternal values of scripture, it will constantly be seeking to develop, remaining appropriate and relevant to its time and location. Like David (Acts 13:36), such churches want to serve the purposes of God in their own generation. "But we've *always* done it this way" are said to be among the last words of the dying church.

The *Raising Families* programme commits to working with local churches for three years. So what happens in years four, five and six? Anecdotally, I had heard many stories of how *RaFa* CAGs and families had continued to thrive, and even multiply, long after the formal training and support processes had ended. But we wanted to establish some more quantifiable evidence of its sustainability, and so in 2016 I began a process by which we could better measure the change and impact of the programme, and its design, organisational quality and sustainability, a process which we called a CIDOS review ('CIDOS' standing for 'Change, Impact, Design, Organisation and Sustainability'). But before we look at the outcomes of this process, let's consider what the scriptures have to say about sustainability and multiplication.

The Biblical Rationale

We could say that generational increase and sustainability is 'in God's image'. *"God created human beings in his own image, in the image of God he created them; male and female he created them. God blessed them and said to them, 'Be fruitful and increase in number...'"* (Genesis 1:27-28 NIV). Three times God made His plan for multiplication clear to Noah when He said, *"Come out of the ark, you and your wife and your sons and their wives. Bring out every kind of living creature that is with you – the birds, the animals, and all the creatures that move along the ground – so they can multiply on the earth and be fruitful and increase in number on it"* (Genesis 8:15-17 NIV), *"Be fruitful and increase in number and fill the earth"* (Genesis 9:1 NIV), and *"As for you, be fruitful and increase in number; multiply on the earth and increase upon it"* (Genesis 9:7 NIV).

However, God's intention for the sustainability and growth of His people, and the consistency of His faithfulness to them, is sadly not matched by His people's response. From the time of Saul to the time of the Assyrian captivity, we read in the Old Testament of forty Kings of Israel and Judah. Only six of them, Asa (I Kings 15:11), Jehoshaphat (I Kings 22:43), Uzziah (2 Chronicles 26:4), Jotham (2 Kings 15:34), Hezekiah (2 Kings 18:3, 5-6) and Josiah (2 Kings 22:2), 'did what was right in the eyes of the Lord', and followed in the ways of their fathers. The remaining thirty four of them (i.e. 85%) either did what was evil, or had at best a chequered history. Maintaining consistency in the blessing and obedience of God from one era to the next was clearly a challenge.

"Good people leave an inheritance for their children's children." Proverbs 13:22 NIV

The odds were just a little better in the New Testament. Although Jesus indicated that 75% of the seed sown (the word) will not bear fruit, the summary point of the story is about the 25% that does bear fruit. "Still other seed fell on good soil. It came up, grew and produced a crop, some multiplying thirty, some sixty, some a hundred times." (Mark 4:8 NIV). So, although many will fall away, due to the excellent return from the minority good crop, the Kingdom will continue not only to be maintained, but also to grow.

When Jesus *"knew that the hour had come for him to leave this world and go to the Father"* (John 13:1 NIV), He also knew that He only had a few brief days for the completion of the face to face mentoring of His disciples before His death on the cross, His resurrection and His ascension into heaven. So what were the final, fundamentally important messages He left with His disciples? Amongst the richness of His teaching in chapters 13-17 of John's gospel, we see some repeated themes. He spoke about servanthood, faithfulness, and of the role of the Holy Spirit. He spoke about Him being the true vine, and He urged them to remain, or abide, in Him (John 15:4-10). So sustainability was uppermost on Jesus' mind. *"All this I have told you so that you will not fall away,"* He said (John 16:1 NIV).

And during that most intense of weeks, when Jesus prayed, He confirmed with His Father that *"none has been lost"* (John 17:12 NIV), something He had earlier discussed with His disciples (John 6:39). And He also prayed generationally when He said to His Father, *"My prayer is not for them alone. I pray also for those who will believe in me through their message"* (John 17:20 NIV).

Paul, in his instruction to Timothy, simply outlines the practical process of discipleship that leads to sustainability and replication. *"You then, my son, be strong in the grace that is in Christ Jesus. And the things you have heard me say in the presence of many* witnesses entrust to reliable people who will also be qualified to teach others" (2 Timothy 2:2 NIV).

In Hebrews 11 we have that famous list of 'ancients', all commended for their faith. There was Abel, Enoch and Noah. And then there was Abraham, from whom *"came descendants as numerous as the stars in the sky and as countless as the sand on the seashore."* (Hebrews 11:12 NIV). Many more examples followed, building up a sense that whilst God was the *object* of their faith, their orientation was on the future. *"All these people were still living by faith when they died. They did not receive the things promised; they only saw them and welcomed them from a distance..."* (Hebrews 11:13 NIV). Women and men of faith are not here for themselves, but are forward-looking, prophetic people who whilst serving their own generation are at the same time always looking beyond their generation for the sake of the Kingdom of God. This is the biblical approach to sustainability and multiplication.

Raising Families Context

In order to specifically test the sustainability of the *RaFa* model we returned to CAGs that had been envisioned and trained by SP partners, but who had received no direct post-programme input for a minimum of twelve months. Some communities revisited had received no direct input for 36 months. To gain external and robust credibility and objectivity in this process, I worked in partnership with Tearfund colleagues to establish a template for our research. In the words of the CIDOS Report Executive Summary, this is what we found.

CIDOS Report, Executive Summary

"Raising Families addresses the root causes of poverty, has a broad impact on the whole person, and the change brought about in families is lasting. Effective change, which does no harm, is brought about at good value for money, and the model's results are causing a stir in the community.

When measuring all these *'change* and *impact'* aspects of the *RaFa* programme, they are demonstrated to be consistently 'strong' (measured as 61-80%).

Results from the survey also demonstrate the 'exceptional strength' (measured as 81-100%) of the *RaFa* programme *'design'* in terms of its commitment to being strongly prayer- and bible-based, and also in the way it addresses the felt needs of the poorest and most marginalised in the communities it serves. The model's design also demonstrates 'strength' by making no financial demands on local churches and communities for central costs, and in the way it addresses structural causes of poverty. Participants are empowered through facilitated adult learning methodology, and the programme, which delivers high technical quality, is replicable and simple to implement.

In terms of the *'organisations'* Samaritan's Purse partners with, the 'exceptional' values and behaviour of the implementing organisations' staff members reinforce a reputation and passion that supports the model's implementation. The implementing organisations learn well, and have good governance and organisational practice, strong monitoring systems and training capacity.

After RaFa has invested into 100 CAGs over three years, the multiplication effect means that on average 158 CAGs will be active in reaching out to their community 18 months after the programme ends.

84% of Church Action Groups (CAGs) still function at least twelve months after *RaFa* support ends. What's more, the survey confirms that not only is the programme *'sustainable'*, but also it is *influential* (77% of the groups testify to the significantly positive influence it has had on their church), it is *transformational* (73% describe the impact of their work on the families they serve as 'transformational'), and that it naturally *multiplies*. From the evidence of this statistical survey, we are able to conclude that after *RaFa* has invested into 100 CAGs over three years, the multiplication effect means on average 158 CAGs will be active in reaching out to their community 18 months after the programme ends.

It had been anticipated that the *impact of pastors moving on* from churches that were envisioned by *RaFa* would be greater than it was. In most surveyed areas of the programme the pastor moving on appears to have had no significant impact on the programme outcomes.

Probably the greatest challenge confirmed through the review is that of *financial sustainability.* 'Financial restraints' was the primary reason given by more than half of the churches that did not continue, and two thirds of the 84% that have continued also claimed that 'financial/resource restraints' has been their main challenge. To address this, the strengthening and earlier introduction of income generating training and initiatives is something *RaFa* has instigated, and will continue to focus on. The report also showed that our implementing organisations tend not to go out of their way to promote the model widely or (particularly) to fundraise for its growth. A more strategic approach is needed by implementing organisations in order to share the model and to seek funds to ensure its future growth.

In conclusion, throughout this report the effectiveness of *Raising Families* can be seen in the excellent *biblical-based vision and capacity* of our partner organisations, the clear vision of their implementing staff as *facilitators*, and the relative *stability* of the nations, communities and church leaderships where it works. The CAGs in turn are effective by their *commitment to the most marginalised* in their communities, and their determination to commit to an *asset-based approach*. Many have reached their high aim of *positively impacting the whole church,* of completing what is described as *'transformational' work with families*, and by their very effective *multiplication into neighbouring communities.* This process has confirmed these strengths, and highlights once more the need for *income generating* to be a key component, both for the partner agencies and for the local communities.

Finally, it must be said that all *RaFa* partners have come through this process with huge credit, and their faith and trust in God, their clear strategic approach, their determination and their hard work is clearly acknowledged in the responses the CAG members and participating families have given when interviewed. Samaritan's Purse UK are very grateful to God for partners with such integrity, skill and experience."[28]

Testimonies from Raising Families Practitioners

---

[28] The full CIDOS report is available. Contact me on my website: CuttingAcross.com

"I have a lot to share"

To a backdrop of a thousand hills, and in the hearing of a hundred villagers, Doroteya and Jean Boscoe shared with me what God had been doing with them.

They have four children, Oliviey (15), Erasto (13), Shadrack (10) and Enoch (9). We heard once more how hard life had been before the *RaFa* training. "We usually had one meal a day, but some days we went without eating at all. It was very hard finding food for the plate. We live in a very small house and had no medical insurance. The government gave some free medical cards to the poorest of the poor, and we were given one of these. But the training gave us sight, and we began to think critically about what we could do. We formed a CAG which meets every Saturday at 2pm to pray, read scripture and save money (350 RWF per week). We began to cultivate our gardens and save the income we generated. We borrowed 5,000 RWF from the savings group and bought and sold tomatoes with it. Then onions, carrots, potatoes and fish. Now we also grow bananas, beans, maize and sweet potatoes, and we bought this little table and scales to make our stall more professional. We also bought two more gardens, a cow, a sheep and ten hens."

"Now we have breakfast, lunch and supper every day. We are all covered by medical insurance which we pay promptly each year ourselves, and the children work much better at school because they are no longer sick and hungry. Our relationship with God has increased. Now we meet together on Sundays, and on Thursdays and Saturdays. Together we talk, we pray, we encourage one another, whereas before we hardly knew each other.

Our relationships within the community have also improved. Our changed lifestyle attracted others in the community to ask questions, and now we encourage other groups to form. After two years we started a second group, and then a third group, affiliated to other confessions, including the Catholic, Seventh Day Adventist, Pentecostal and Anglican churches. The groups are called The Blessed, The United and The Oneness."

I asked Doroteya what advice she would give to a struggling family these days. She smiled. "I have a lot to share with such people." she said. "They need not be defeated and pathetic any more. They can borrow 5,000 RFW, and if they use it wisely they will soon have a cow, use the manure to grow better crops, and things will grow for them from there."

"I've started five other groups"

Emelienne lives with her husband and six children in a rural village in Rwanda. She shared her transformational story outside her mud-brick house.

Before her church received envisioning and training through the *Raising Families* programme, their lives could only be described as hopeless. Finding food and school fees was a real challenge and all her children suffered some form of malnutrition. Having no funds to pay for health insurance, they were excluded from even the most basic of health care, and rather than being an income generator, the fruit from her garden's two lemon trees was casually picked and eaten by random passers-by.

However, just over three years ago Emelienne was sent as representative of her church to a *Raising Families* training. She returned to her village envisioned and motivated, and immediately set up a Church Action Group of seven members. Determined to see transformation in their neighbourhood, they assessed the community's needs and assets, and then committed to supporting 20 of the most vulnerable families in the village. Together they met every two weeks to pray, read scripture and save together to raise funds that will help these families lift themselves out of poverty.

"When we were trained on recognising and using our assets, I realised I could harvest the lemons from my two lemon trees. I netted 5,000 RWF (£5) from the first harvest, and realised that if I could multiply the number of trees I had, then my income would grow. So I borrowed from the savings group and bought 22 more lemon trees. We're now on our third harvest and each harvest brings in 50,000 RWF (£50). I gave some lemon seedlings to my neighbours and trained them up. Then I buy back their produce and sell it in the market, together with their banana, avocado and tomato harvests. God has blessed us simply and abundantly, and all from what we already had!"

"The training was more than eye-opening; it was revolutionary! As a result of these initiatives my children go to school, their diet has improved, and we all have medical insurance."

Emelienne has now started five other cross-denominational church action groups and the impact is being multiplied. After saving regularly out of their own pockets these groups are now investing livestock into the vulnerable families they serve, they're building new homes for the destitute and their community is taking note.

"This year alone in our little village we have 12 new believers and 10 others have returned to their faith. This is our encouragement to carry on working hard. God says in Revelation 2:9, 'I know about your suffering and poverty, but you are rich!' This is so true, and now we've been challenged with this we're joining with Paul in 2 Corinthians 6:10 and saying, 'We are poor, yet we are bringing spiritual riches to others.'"

When it's time to leave the nest

Some Church Action Group leaders from Kyrgyzstan share their thoughts on going it alone.

"When Samaritan's Purse finished working with us I had a feeling of confusion and loneliness, because we are used to receiving good support from you. But then I realised that our time to become independent had come. It was time to use all the knowledge that we received from you. So little by little we started moving on, and today our team continues not only to serve poor people in our community, but also we share our experience with other churches." *Pastor B, Kyrgyzstan.*

"We regularly have this tremendous sense of gratitude to Samaritan's Purse for the *RaFa* process that you implemented in our community. You taught us that we could serve the community more effectively. When the time came to leave, there was no fear at all, as we were prepared for 'independence'. All the knowledge and experience that we received helps us today in our work as a Church Action Group. Realising that it was not only us for whom the work was complete, and that other CAGs were also feeling a little vulnerable, we decided to establish an Association of all the other CAGs that we had trained with, in order to help and support each other for ongoing and more effective work in their communities." *A, Kyrgyzstan.*

"Immediately after the end of your work with us we experienced fear and uncertainty, wondering who would support us now. Then we calmed down, and relied only on the Lord. We had to recall everything that we were taught during training, began to conduct fundraising companies to continue working with disabled children in our Rehabilitation Center, and built very good relations with local state structures. Today we are boldly looking to the future, *"being confident of this very thing, that He who has begun a good work in you will perform it until the day of Jesus Christ."* Philippians 1:6." *AA, Kyrgyzstan.*

"When the work on the programme was completed, as a pastor I had to take responsibility for further work. There was no fear. Instead there was a determination to grow, and to serve the community in which we live, using the knowledge and experience we gained from your organisation. Thank you very much for you ministry to us". *Pastor T, Kyrgyzstan.*

Questions for Group Discussion

- What have I done today that will create a positive legacy for the future?
- Discuss how discipleship, equipping and mentoring actively take place in our church.
- What are the attitudes and practices in my life that will hinder growth and sustainability?
- What is the greatest legacy you can leave for others after you have gone?
- How often do you pray for the future of your children, your grandchildren, and for future generations of descendants that you might never personally meet?

- 'Doers' impact the present generation, whereas the impact of 'equippers' is for several generations. Discuss.

Where to go from here

I am very conscious of the fact that UK church leaders and activists wanting to act on some of these lessons will have to take a large contextual leap in order to apply them to their UK neighbourhoods. I have condensed some of the contents of the book into a format suitable for a church weekend, or a training series, and am available for the leading or facilitating of such events. Please contact me on my website, **CuttingAcross.com**, for further discussion and correspondence regarding this.

About the Author

For 20 years, Alan Cutting was a pastor and church-planter. In more recent years his primary role has been to envision and equip churches across the world. These days he is available as a speaker, trainer and consultant on church and community development. Alan enjoys international travel, family history, and watching non-league football.

CuttingAcross.com is Alan's website. On it you can find his other publications, blogs and videos, as well as photos he has taken around the world, and podcasts of talks he has given. Contact him on his website with your comments, suggestions, questions and requests.

Other books by Alan Cutting

Cutting Across the Borders

"My story leads you through my nervous but rescued childhood. It opens a door into the intensive community lifestyle that I lived in my twenties and thirties. And it tussles with the pain, betrayal and disasters that I encountered during my forties. And the rest is geography. I invite you to journey with me on the relentless, unusual and often extreme global adventures of my fifties and sixties.

It's a story of people, of places and of relationships; a true and radical tale of love and passion, of disappointment, vulnerability and determination. And of rescue and grace, hope and faithfulness."

Alan Cutting

47119578R00146

Printed in Poland
by Amazon Fulfillment
Poland Sp. z o.o., Wrocław